The Inspired Folly

The Inspired Folly

Nancy Pence Britton

Illustrated by
John Strickland Goodall

William Blackwood
Edinburgh & London
1971

William Blackwood & Sons Ltd
45 George Street
Edinburgh EH2 2JA

Set in Monotype Series 2 Old Style and Series 239 Perpetua
Italic and printed at the Press of the Publisher, William
Blackwood & Sons Ltd, Edinburgh

ISBN : 0 85158 107 2

Contents

What is life but a series of inspired follies?

G. B. Shaw, *Pygmalion*

We Approach the Ideal

Fate appears to have the best intentions.

Saki, *The Unbearable Bassington*

The reason why Frank and I were driving down from London to Bristol that fine Friday afternoon in July was so ingrained in us both that we could have done it standing on our heads. Maybe it would have worked out better if we had. We were making for unknown territory, whose possible merits or faults as a community were wholly unrelated to the issue, to find, with all speed and no fuss, the best available living space for the two of us, near Frank's job, for an indefinite spell.

This was a routine we had danced through with a minimum of stress some twenty times already, since that happy day long ago when the Museum of Fine Arts in Boston, Massachusetts, had sent me to Cairo to write a book, and I had fetched up almost accidentally, over Christmas, in Khartoum Cathedral, a thousand miles to the south, merging my heart and passport with Frank's along the primrose flarepath of the Royal Air Force. We had found places to live in Egypt, Canada and Malaya, with stop-overs of varying brevity in the less likely by-ways of England and Wales. These dwellings were never featured in *House and Garden*, but for us they all had a rugged charm.

In the Cairo *pension* which we first fleetingly called home, my minuscule Russian landlady, taking sights on Frank's height, murmured that she would borrow an outsize bed from a friend's shop-window. (As my French is never very strong, I got the fixed idea that we were to sleep *in* the shop-window.) At Ismailia, our vulnerable door locks and balconies were defended, in theory anyway, by the cook's cousin sleeping on the doormat. In the cottage in Wales, luxury stopped short at a wood range and the tin bath we dragged near it, but ours were the only windows in the village that went up and down, on kitchen weights. In sub-zero Ottawa, the landlord provided twenty-seven Buddhas but no blankets. At Camberley, mice entered through the fireplace and exited under the French windows. In Singapore, the nine unglazed windows circling our main room ensured that during the monsoons the carpet got

2

wet evenly all over. In the Nissen hut on Salisbury Plain, the hanging of pictures endangered the outside structure, and a bowl of flowers on the dining-room table lasted through the winter, preserved in a block of ice. In our next abode, a nearby thatched cottage, Frank bore a permanent head-wound from the low beams. And for other English stop-overs, we had rescued so many stables that it had been suggested we should have been voted honorary fellows of the R.S.P.C.A.

In other words, we were not what you would call hidebound house-hunters. Having never in our married life had to stay in one place for less than three weeks or more than three years, we viewed real estate with a less carping eye than if we were liable to be stuck with the product for life. Our ideal was something small, well-built, centrally placed, labour-saving and sunny, with a dash of style and a nice garden. But, in this imperfect world, we weren't too proud, however short the lease, to re-mould the Available nearer to the Heart's Desire by providing, with our own cash and fingernails, some such missing detail as a system of plumbing or heating, or a new house-wall if the old one fell down, or a hand-laid patio, or a trellis of thorniest roses. And, once only, Frank reluctantly re-erected for me a full-grown tree that I found by the roadside. The tree, he pointed out, would have been bushier and prettier if it could be planted root-side up.

Our zeal for improving other people's property, which should have made us the landlords' darlings, never brought us even a thank-you from this

3

grudging tribe, maybe because we couldn't wait for it before moving on, and we sometimes paused to query the wisdom of a programme of perennial tenancy, however joyous and full of healthful exercise. It wasn't that we were against house-buying in principle. It was just that, in practice, by some natural law, someone else's redeemable building always turned up in the nick of time.

We assumed that this law would still be in force on our present excursion, in spite of one trivial amendment to last season's rules, hardly worth mentioning: that this time we would operate as civilians, Frank having just been offered a plummy job in a Bristol aircraft firm, for which he was applying to leave the R.A.F. as soon as con-venient. But as an attraction of the new job, other than the novel presence of money, lay in its exact resemblance to Service life (including vague terms of reference, insecure tenure, heady hints at an imminent change of base, and, meantime, the assumption by all hands that, at the signal, any man would dash anywhere in the world, ready to stay a day or a month as occasion suggested), we foresaw no troublesome adjustment to civilian life, and no need to mess up our housing habits. So our plan was to drive to Bristol for the night, line up a house by Saturday tea-time, and continue to Frank's gardening aunt in Devon for the week-end.

Neither of us had been to Bristol before. Well, Frank had gone down for interview earlier in the week, but he said he hadn't seen much because a Company car met him off the train and took him

4

by side roads to the Works and back again. "Blindfolded?" I asked. "Unfortunately no," was all he replied. This didn't upset either of us, as the disarray of a town in its station environs wasn't our problem. The sun still shone, and the landscape to westward was obligingly studded with Palladian mansions and picture-book villages.

Late in the day Frank, who was driving, said he presumed this sudden paralysis of traffic and the total absence of road signs must indicate the approach of Bristol and, handing me a giant accordion map which I had never set eyes on before, he said to give him quickly the best route into town. I told him this was a touching expression of faith, as he must know that I am no navigator. But after an agony of unfolding, I ventured that we might creep in from the north, where there was a big open space, maybe a park. Frank, dodging between a tanker and an articulated lorry, asked tersely if my park might be Filton Aerodrome. I found it was. He then wanted to know precisely where we were *now*. Beating down the map to see the road, I had to confess I wasn't sure, but I said if we turned right at the next corner we couldn't go wrong. After making the turn, he commented that I had at least shaken off the traffic. This was undeniable, especially after the tarred road changed to gravel, and the last of the cars still with us peeled off into farm-yards. The road, by now a dirt track, turned a blind corner through a muddy ford, made a U-turn onto a broken bridge and, with protean versatility, shrank into a mad little lane burrowing frantically uphill, smothered in brambles and engulfed in wild hedges.

Eventually Frank said my road seemed to have no plan in life except survival, and asked where we were, and I was just protesting that it wasn't *my* road, and that according to *his* map we didn't exist at all, when we bumped over a tangled hillock and were emptied onto the verge of a great eminence, with the glory of Bristol bursting beneath us, not to the south where she belonged, but full to the north-west in the blaze of a gaudy sunset.

The river ran crimson, and smokestacks billowed flamingo pink, and the streets were so crazed with little harbour inlets that ships nuzzled houses, and masts nudged chimney-pots and Gothic spires, all awash in a gauzy haze. The thickly housed slopes that rimmed the city, rising ridge upon gentle ridge, were hung with strings of rosy window-panes like sugar-plums. Up above, a thin silver bridge floated free in the sky, and from behind, a mass of mountains moved in taller and darker to meet the heavy sun.

" Glory hallelujah! " I breathed, overcome by a magic too romantic to bear.

" Nice, isn't it? " Frank said complacently. I giggled lightheadedly and told him he sounded as if he were patting the head of a very large dog. " Friendly, we hope," he contributed. And as we moved slowly down the precipitous road into Bristol, I got involved in an anecdote about a gentle-eyed Great Dane I once knew in Cambridge, Massachusetts, who bit strangers while still giving a come-on with a wagging tail.

6

By the time we had lined up a hotel room, we had learned quite a bit about Bristol. We had come down off our eminence and, considering how few things in life look quite as well close up, had found the city holding her charms pretty well, if in an offhand schizophrenic manner, tugged two ways by the glorious past and the expedient present.

Take the Church of St Mary Redcliffe, once admired by the first Queen Elizabeth. There it stood, its crockets and ballflowers soaring serenely above the evening dock traffic, and almost rubbing buttresses with the sooty railway station.

Farther on, Queen Square's fluted-shell door-hoods and Regency balconies, and the over-rich Stuart and Georgian elegance of King Street, were relieved by some tatty modern warehouses. And to top the lot, across from the Cathedral, where a massive Norman arch supported a lacy Gothic tower, a stout marble Queen Victoria gazed forever beady-eyed towards where the tiny unique medieval Mayor's Chapel was concealed by some post-war shop-fronts of truly inspired tawdriness.

Another thing we had deduced was that there was nothing we could usefully do that night about finding a house. The humming centre of Bristol, where our hotel lay, was so clearly dedicated solely to the concept of Doing rather than just Living, and the crowds that filled the streets on our arrival had, at pack-up time, vanished so rapidly down some plug-hole, leaving behind the silence of sudden disaster, that we felt the workers must be powerfully drawn, for their nightly revelries, to even better outlying rose-hung colonies which would be revealed to us in the morning.

Our third conclusion was that it would be wiser to eat out. This view, prompted by the boiled cabbage which already made its presence felt throughout the hotel, was backed by the hall porter whose advice we sought. Glancing behind the potted palms for spies, he confided that the mutton had been on for two days running, and that there was a good fish restaurant not five minutes away, we couldn't miss it. Well, as it happened, we could miss it, and Frank said the block-time for the course couldn't be less than ten minutes, even for a well-briefed crow, depending of course on its cruising speed. But when we found it, it was worth it.

So that after a meal of local fresh lobster, accompanied by a good Bristol sherry and followed by West Country cheeses, we sat well back from the table, warming our brandy glasses, reviewing the day's events, planning for the morrow, and wondering which of the glittering strings of sugar-plum windows that we had viewed from our eminence that afternoon would be ours by this time tomorrow.

As we strolled out into the streets, on a circular tour toward our hotel (we hoped), past the Corinthian façade of the Corn Exchange, and The Nails (hence ' Pay on the nail '), past the octagonal cupola of All Saints, white against the blue sky, and the prim spire of Christ Church, and the bulging walls of the Rummers' Inn, and the shuttered market, and under the clock-tower of the old city wall, the late summer daylight was paling. In the city centre where, earlier, a stream of motorcars had looped a furious cat's-cradle around two oases of bright marigolds, the streets were now empty. The yellow arc-lights had come on, muting the bright flowers to dun and puce. The traffic lights changed endlessly from red to yellow to green and back to red again, and the marble Victoria stared crossly into shifting neon shop-signs. Down a steep vista of buildings, the moon-whitened skeletons of churches blitzed in the Nazi raids cast long black shadows onto the ground-mists, and ships hooted in the loneliness.

We went to bed early and slept well.

Visions of Sugar Plums

The children were nestled all snug in their beds
While visions of sugar-plums danced through
their heads.

Clement Moore, *The Night Before
Christmas* (December 1823)

Next morning we started on the house agents,
chosen not for any known merit but because they
were in the biggest print in the classified phone
book. But Frank suggested that first we should
cruise about in the car for a bit, to see some of the
outlying beauty spots and decide which district
we preferred to live in.

"What beauty spots?" I asked him an hour

later, after we had circled the suburbs by a web of mean little streets wedged with shabby house-fronts and swept by a dusty wind bearing cigarette wrappers. Frank said Bristol did seem to have shot her bolt with the city centre and gone quietly to pieces elsewhere. I asked him if he had decided which district he preferred to live in, and he said preferably none that he had yet seen.

The first agent had only one house listed, and we went along to see it. It had five floors, a basement kitchen, a bath-geyser on a landing, stained glass in the front hall, ivy over the windows, what looked like deadly nightshade in the front yard, and a whiff of something indefinable throughout. Two wizened sisters, Arsenic and Old Lace, wouldn't do business unless we bought the horsehair sofa, the carpet with the holes, and all the brass bedsteads, including the one which, they mentioned gaily, papa had died in.

We were firmer with the second agent. We insisted on a description of his houses before we went to view them. He said he didn't have any houses to describe. We asked if he had any mewses. He said, " What's that when it's at home? " We said a mews was a sort of stable or coach-house, and he laughed his head off and said that Bristol was a modern city and hadn't used horses or coaches for years. He said he could show us a two-room flat over an undertaker with use of W.C., but we said, " Not at this stage," and left. Long afterwards we learned that there are some mewses in Clifton.

The third agent, when we could draw him from

a cosy phone chat with a lady-friend which sounded fraught with promise, also had nothing to offer. Neither did the fourth, fifth and sixth agents. I asked Frank how so many Bristol estate agents could subsist with nothing to sell, and he said they must play the horses.

The seventh agent said didn't we know there was a housing shortage? Frank replied that he was beginning to suspect it. At that we broke off for a quick one, which we badly needed by then, at a nearby pub, and we had a couple of cardboard sandwiches to go with it, to save time over lunch.

Then we tried another agent, one we had noticed earlier, not on our list, whose window was stuffed with pictures of houses to enable the passer-by to know the worst without going in. However, inside, the agent said he wouldn't advise our fooling with any of these, as a property had to be proved unsaleable for some months before the owner took the grim step of paying to have it photographed. He said his latest hot-off-the-griddle offers were concealed in " this file ", which he tapped significantly, and then hastened to spoil his build-up by examining each card in turn and shaking his head sadly. This discouraging ritual was interrupted by a phone ringing in the back room, which he went off to answer, and when he returned, we could offer *him* several possibilities, which he greeted with little happy cries. So off we all went on a treasure hunt in our car.

For the first of the possibles, of the semi-detached shoebox school, we didn't even slow down as we could smell it from the road. But the second one was a real car-stopper, squeezed in between a couple of tall houses, and overflowing its plot with obtuse angles. " Different," the agent summed it up, scanning us brightly for reactions. Then, perusing the card, he fell back in a rapture and said the house was designed and built by a university professor. " Of architecture?" Frank asked. The agent said no, and named an unrelated subject. I said I shouldn't have thought he'd have time for house-designing.

Before we even rang the doorbell the wife joined us on the step and held us there bodily, extolling with vivacity and just a shade of desperation the treat in store for us, using the word ' ultra-modern ' three times, and stressing that the only reason she could wrench herself from this ultimate in homes was that the professor had designed and built a second house, equipped with a bigger study. When she let go and allowed us in, we soon saw that her husband was well advised to break off and try again, because his first attempt had left a trail of doors that stuck and floors that creaked and taps that dripped and stairs that sagged and ceilings that leaked ever so slightly. The ultra-modern note was struck by a lone radiator in the front hall, fed by the kitchen range behind the wall and, in the living-room, by a picture-window overlooking the dustbins in a tiny cement yard. She was willing to let or sell, and the prices she quoted would allow for gold-leafing the professor's new study. We thanked her politely and fled.

Back in the car, Frank asked the agent how to

get to the next house on our list. "But didn't you like this house?" the agent asked forlornly. I thought he was going to cry. We had to tell him as gently as we could that we didn't. Frank asked him again how to get to the next house. At this, the agent lost interest. He said they had only been given the house the day before, that they hadn't seen it, that the owners were away for the week-end and hadn't left a key and, when pressed, that the question of the agent's fee hadn't been entirely ironed out yet. Frank said well we could at least see the outside of the house, and why not get on with it?

This involved manipulating the car up a steep little zigzag road, and, at the top, backing into a minute turnabout overhanging a cliff. By the time I had eased on my shoes and caught up with the men behind the house, Frank was balanced on the rail of a small rustic patio peering in at the living-room window. "This is a fairly habitable structure," he exclaimed to me in surprise. I climbed up and looked in too. It was a fine big room, defaced by a dreadful fireplace, a brown dado, and a quantity of bulbous furniture, but with generous windows on three sides and a French door to the garden.

We made a slow tour of the outside of the house, looking in where we could. Artistically it was no great shakes. Every inch of its two storeys shrieked the date 1908 that was carved into the plaque over the front door. (Frank asked the agent what cataclysm had hit Bristol in 1908 that compelled total rebuilding, and the agent replied that he couldn't say; he was a Bath man himself.) But whether it was that by then my critical sense was blunted, or that the house's rather stingy proportions were enveloped in a luscious cloud of pink clematis, or that, best of all, the ugly little box stood sturdily above a small slope of lawns and flower-beds, with a screen of shrubbery at the wall and dizzy little glimpses of the bustling city visible far below between the branches; whatever the combination of causes, I felt the familiar mounting excitement that had spiced life for me in various parts of the globe. " I could live here, darling," I said. Frank said he could too. Turning briskly to the agent, he said we would have the house, subject to survey and contract. The agent looked frankly appalled. " But you haven't seen inside yet," he protested. He added primly that no action could be taken that day because of the owners' absence, and that he would advise us to go away and consider the matter very carefully. He said we could contact the owners on Monday if we were still interested.

On the way down he asked piteously if we would care for another peek at the professor's house. We broke it to him that we would not. When we had dropped him at his office, I commented to Frank that this agent was trying to sell us the wrong house.

We tried a few more estate offices on the way back to the hotel, but didn't strike another spark. Anyway, as Frank said, we had already found what we wanted. So we picked up our bags from the lobby and headed for Devon.

Tia, Frank's aunt, was one of the unscheduled bonuses of my marriage. She was a frail five-foot-one, pushing eighty years old, with Dresden china colouring, a Nefertiti profile, a lordly manner and the strength of a horse. When we arrived, she was presiding at tea, wearing, slightly askew, the battered wide-brimmed gardening hat which she affected indoors and out, and distributing cups and conversation to four admiring spade-bearded Continental experts who had come to see her garden.

When these eventually bowed from her presence, with the kissing of hands, and she got down to our affairs, she didn't think it in the least odd that we should buy a house without stepping inside it, as house interiors never interested her greatly any-how. Her chief concern, she told us, nimbly seizing my half-full tea cup, which I had been trying to conceal, and handing it back quivering to the brim with the scalding black brew—*our* chief concern, she amended graciously, would be to root up instantly the long vigorous well-tended borders of hollyhocks, lupins and other vulgar herbaceous stuff which we had been describing to her with some enthusiasm, and to replace them with little-known shrubs from the Levant or the lower reaches of the Himalayas, none of which had names of less than five syllables, and all of which, she readily agreed, would take many pleasant years to mature, assuming they survived at all outside the fruity soil of Devon.

Early Sunday morning she had us roused and summoned to her room where, while breakfasting in bed (a fetching lace mob-cap replaced the gardening hat), she was compiling long lists of obscure plants, which she proposed transferring bodily from her garden to ours the minute we said the word (assuming we could pronounce it).

By lunchtime we were calling that ugly little box on the hill " Our House ", and had mentally dismantled the fireplace, repainted the dado, revamped the kitchen and pantry, and perhaps removed a few upstairs walls. Frank proposed a bigger garage and a wider turnabout. Tia said, " Is that wise, dear? Can we spare space from the garden? " We left for Bristol at dawn Monday, waved off absently by Tia, who was impressing on us to ask the owners the names of the shrubs lining the boundary wall and to drop her a post-card.

My fear, which I had been repeating with monotonous regularity, that the house would have been snapped up in our absence, proved groundless. We phoned from the first Bristol call-box we saw, and the owner, a small thin elderly voice, said he and his wife were just back from Kent, and why didn't we phone again in a few days? When he heard we were on our way back to London, he agreed indifferently to our going around then.

The voice was attached to a spry little man with a nice plump rosy wife, both of them very chatty, not about this house, which they seemed to find boring, but about the hop-farm they were retiring to. The inside of the house was as comfortably old-fashioned as we had expected, but the basic lines were good, and the views, especially upstairs, were breathtaking. Frank tapped the wall between two of the tiny bedrooms and nodded to me, repeating the process downstairs between the kitchen and larder. The owner asked with alert amusement if we were looking for buried treasure, and Frank grinned back that we were.

Before we left, we said we would buy the house at their price (which was about half the professor's), subject to survey and contract, and that we would stop off and fix it with the agent. The couple just laughed and shrugged incredulously, and we shook hands all round, " to seal it ", as Frank told them. As we dashed down the hill, it hit me that I hadn't asked those shrub names for Tia, but Frank said it was just as well, as they looked too big to dig up if she didn't like them.

The agent was just hanging up his hat when we appeared, and he acted as if we were the bearers of bad rather than good tidings. But when Frank directly asked him, he named an independent Bristol surveyor and agreed to get him out to the house that day without fail and to have him report to us at once by phone or letter. When Frank took out his cheque book to make a deposit, the agent waved it away gloomily and said it was still early days.

As we bowled off toward London, I remarked fatuously that we seemed to have acquired a place to live. " That was the object of the exercise," Frank observed mildly.

The Degree of Encouragement

> Providence seldom vouchsafes to mortals any more than just that degree of encouragement which suffices to keep them at a reasonably full exertion of their powers.
>
> Hawthorne, *The Scarlet Letter*

All this time we should have been relaxing in the South of France. Frank's leave had been due to start a week before. But when the Bristol job cropped up, we scrubbed everything and settled for a long week-end locally, Friday to Wednesday, to sort things out.

One of these things was to find a sub-tenant for our London mews, which for some years had been our closest approach to a home base. We had come by it in a quaint way. A few weeks after the end of the war, we had converged on London from far distances after long separation (Frank from the Middle East, I from the Waves in Washington), and during a sentimental prowl of our favourite haunts, snooping through a noble old archway back of Regent's Park, part of the Nash Terraces, we had come upon a half-bombed Regency stable and coach-house, minus one wall and teetering on the edge of a crater. An aged road-sweeper said it was Crown property. So on a rumour, soon after, that Frank was to be posted to London, we wrote to the Crown agents, asking if we could have all or part of it to do up as a cottage.

To this we had no reply. Until, two years and three moves later, a letter, forwarded on by leisurely country post offices, reached us in Bedford, written by the Crown agents as if we had applied to them only yesterday ('In reply to your request for a lease on a Crown mews property . . .'), and offering us the whole little shebang, coach-house and stable, on a seven-year lease, for peppercorn rent plus rates, we to pay for rebuilding the fallen wall and converting the ruin from horses to people; *and* giving us a deadline, only thirty-six hours away, for acceptance! As this date coincided with our take-off on another Continental holiday, we speeded up our plans, kept the phone humming all day, packed late that night, and spent the next day in London, rounding up surveyors, architects and builders, and leaving them to argue it out with the Crown agents, while we dashed for the airport.

Many agonising and expensive months later (during which our architects dissolved partnership, leaving us up a gum tree with a peevish builder, all of us unenthusiastic about architects), the result of our efforts was the tiny, trim, centrally-heated, lofty-beamed two-bedroom cottage with garage and postage-stamp garden, to which we were returning from Bristol, and which over the years had given us delight and security quite disproportionate to its size. When we were in London, we lived in it; when in the country, we used it for week-ends; when we were overseas, we sub-let it. It had of course been the cause of occasional heartburn to us. At the death of King George VI (' Party of the First Part ' in our lease) we feared for the validity of our tenure, but all was well, and Queen Elizabeth II made the most glamorous new landlady imaginable, though she didn't come around with the rent book personally. Another moment of heart-failure was when our seven-year lease expired, and the agents dug in their heels and declined to give us a written renewal; but they wrote back soothingly that things would continue exactly as before ' for the foreseeable future '. And indeed it had been the happiest arrangement.

What we needed was a short sub-let, six months to a year, to help the mews pay for itself while we shot the rapids of moving to Bristol; so Frank, on the eve of our Bristol trip, had written the Crown agents one of his usual courtesy notes describing the position. And there on the doormat on our return was what we assumed was another of their usual acknowledgements. But it wasn't. It was a body blow. They had a new broom in, whom we had never heard of, who was changing all the rules on us. The foreseeable future had after all been unforeseeable and had caught up with us. From that moment on there were to be no more sub-lets. No more pegged rents. (Cottages with central-heating, such as we had paid for installing, were particularly heavily penalised.) And to top the lot, they said that on our departure (which they were doing their sweet best to hasten) they would expect us to cough up a hefty sum to redecorate the place, inside and out. This last cut us to the quick, as we were those silly-billies who had kept up the Forth Bridge sort of task of maintaining our place spick and span, to the derision of our more feckless neighbours, with their peeling paint and nailed-on, orange-crate repairs. The letter ended by asking us to apprise them of our desires. At that moment, mine were unprintable.

Frank phoned the Crown agents straightaway to debate a few points tactfully. But as he had the bad luck to get the New Broom, who had extra stiff bristles that day, and who kept referring to himself rather conceitedly as The Crown, and since it takes two to make a debate anyway, this wasn't very productive. When Frank delicately reminded him of the several thousand pounds sterling we had spent on improving a bomb-site, and asked what refund we could expect on our exit, the Broom replied baldly that it was not The Crown's policy to refund sums to tenants. From this tactical stronghold, the Broom ended the one-sided jousting match by saying he would continue the discussion with our solicitor. Here was a mortal jab. The Crown agents knew darn well by this time that we didn't *have* a tame solicitor. Never having had problems of any size before, we had deprived ourselves of that cosy one-upman relationship.

We sought to remedy this. We put on our hats, and out we went, and soon found one, around the corner over an invisible mending shop. And while this solicitor's empty do-it-yourself waiting-room and uncluttered desk seemed to hint that he was perhaps not the most sought-after member of his profession, he must at least have been keen enough for clients, one would have thought, to pursue our case avidly for what there was in it for him. But not a bit of it. When we had outlined our problem, he just sat there regarding us as if he had caught us spitting on the flag; and in a rich baritone, sufficiently resonant to make the invisible menders below drop a stitch, he proclaimed, " You cannot sue the Queen! " For this he charged us five guineas, cash on the spot, no cheques. On our way down the dark rickety stairs, Frank, who is resilient, suddenly chuckled and said you could set it to music: " Rule, Britannia! You cannot sue the Queen! "

And while it didn't seem to us that the Crown came into it, directly or indirectly, and we were still inordinately fond and proud of the beautiful, hard-working Queen, and we cheered louder than anybody if she rode by, our immediate reaction to our troubles was that we were fed to the teeth with all landlords and landladies and their little whims, and we were jolly glad we had *bought* the house in Bristol, and could make our own rules this time.

Early Tuesday morning the phone rang. Frank took the call downstairs and came up to report. " The surveyor? " I cried, a bundle of anxiety. Frank looked amused. He said no, it was the London head of an Edinburgh firm who wanted to publish my book about Singapore. I was dumfounded. The manuscript in question was a bantam-weight account of our R.A.F. tour in Malaya, which I had been fussing over much too long, and which, only the previous week, to clear the decks for our move, I had bundled off to a London agent. His instant reaction had been that since it was written in Americanese, he proposed sending it to their New York branch, who could speak the patois. That the thing should have sidetracked to Edinburgh so quickly, and that the code had been cracked by the Scots, added zest to the whole adventure. Frank said the chap on the phone sounded very civilised. (This seemed to surprise him.) He added that I was invited to drop in at the London office around eleven. I asked him if he would come too. He said he wouldn't miss it for worlds.

Our next phone call was from a bloke in Air Ministry, regarding Frank's application for release, to say that Frank's interpretation of ' as soon as convenient ' (' several weeks ') didn't tally with their version: ' up to six months '. I could hear Frank hit the ceiling. But after some good-humoured dickering, they whittled the difference to mid-September. This involved Frank in a drawn-out trunk call to Bristol, to try and trace his future boss, who eventually turned out to be in London for the day. Frank tracked him down, and got invited to lunch. Then it was time for us to leave for the publishers.

With one thing and another, it was past three when Frank's taxi and mine met up outside our mews, I loaded with shopping bags, he with a load of cheer from his lunch party, and we caught our breath and realised we hadn't heard from Bristol about the house. First we rang through to the house agent, where an adenoidal girl said her boss was out for the day and *she* didn't know anything about it. Then we tried the surveyor's office, and when there was no answer at all, we told each other that he must be out at Our House, crawling through the drains.

It turned out that Frank's glow from the lunch party was not all alcoholic. He had been bucked also by his boss's airy acceptance of the mid-September date, and his rosy outline of Frank's duties: " China one week, Peru the next." I told him this all sounded very jolly, but what was I supposed to be doing while he put the world in his pocket? He advised me not to cross the Great Wall of China till we came to it. That evening we toasted several things in a half-bottle of champagne from the wine bin under the stairs.

It was the next morning, Wednesday, before Frank left for work, that the knockout came. A brief note from the surveyor informed us that since the property we were interested in had been sold to another purchaser, ' it had not been necessary ' for him to examine it for us! Handing me this remarkable document, Frank went and rang through to the house agent, was told by Adenoids that he was engaged, and told her to tell him to disengage himself *now*, which happened in record time. The agent confirmed the surveyor's news, saying that neighbours of the owners had topped our price the very day we were there; that this was quite in order and we had no complaint; but that it was *not* in order for the owners to decline to pay him an agent's fee. (He clearly found this the only upsetting feature of the affair.) He added hopefully that the professor's house was still free. Frank said he felt sure it would be, and rang off.

We sat there without saying anything, feeling utter Charleys. I said, "Darling, it was an awfully ugly little house." Frank said. "It would have been hell driving up and down that hill in winter." I said, "I don't think Tia would have liked those shrubs." Frank didn't say anything. I said, "I'm miserable about it, aren't you?" Frank said yes, he was. Then he had to go off to work.

So we started all over again.

We Daren't Go A-Hunting

Up the airy mountain, down the rushy glen,
We daren't go a-hunting for fear of little men.

William Allingham, *The Fairies*

This time round we went at it a trifle grimly,
drained of our first dewy enthusiasm, but determined to find a ruddy place to live, preferably
without being pushed about by any more quaint
lovable West Country characters. To this end we
called into play techniques we had reserved in the
past for hard-nut communities. We didn't plan to
take things quite as far as one couple we knew,
who assessed the housing market by circularising

27

the divorce courts and funeral parlours. But we didn't dismiss it from the scheme of things that we might have to cultivate a lot of postmen, milkmen and dustmen before we were safely householders again. We also recalled that we had got one Singapore house from a grocery shop.

Our first steps were more orthodox. Having time to play with, with Frank's release-date put back to mid-September, we ordered from our London newsagent one issue of every newspaper in the Bristol area, and never can a countryside have been so rich in reading matter. We replied to each house ad. that looked promising, enclosing a stamped envelope. We didn't hear back from a single one.

We chose the most promising of these newspapers and put in an ad. of our own. This brought nothing either.

We also bought a Bristol classified phone book, no mean feat when tackled in London, which could supply directories for New York, Tokyo or Singapore, but had yet to be convinced of Bristol's existence. From this phone book we took two columns of house agents and sent to every blessed one of them a form-letter with our requirements. Then we sat and waited. And waited. And waited. Nothing happened.

Then we bought another sheet of postage stamps and sent a form-letter reminding everybody. This effected a leak in the dyke. A few answers trickled in, mostly without the slightest resemblance to our requirements. Three agents offered the professor's house. Another house sounded perfect until we found it was forty miles from Bristol.

From then on nothing stirred. We reviewed the position like a couple of generals trying to win a war from back at base with blank cartridges, and we had to admit we were plumb out of ammunition to jolt this resistant city by remote control, and we would have to wait and tackle it from some nearby hotel after Frank started work. We were not unduly worried. We always *had* found a place to live, and assumed we would this time without bursting a blood vessel over it. I said why bother with a house anyway? I *liked* hotels. Frank said he liked some hotels too in moderation, but the ones he had seen in Bristol were not among these, and he couldn't picture us happy or solvent like that for long. He said he was going to forget the whole subject until we could do something practical about it. I said me too.

This should have been easy, as we both had plenty on our plates. I was in a pleasant flurry of arrangements about the book; Frank's release from the Air Force, which had been slipping back gradually, was officially taped for the end of September, and he was busy tying in the ends; and there was all the paper-work for handing back the mews, and the packing to plan out. But somehow this time housing didn't expunge itself at all helpfully. It kept bobbing up and intruding, a lively ghost beckoning us down unsuitable alleys.

When, one day, we dodged a sudden rainshower by sheltering in the doorway of an empty Oxford Street shop, we found it taken over by a government housing-exhibition, urging us to accept a public grant for dividing any old wreck of a house into two or more self-contained dwellings. For a couple of sample cases they quoted grants of five hundred pounds and a thousand pounds. Frank's only reaction was that he could see why taxes were so high. But before the rain let up, I was suggesting, in fun you understand, that we should hurry back to Bristol and buy up the Deadly Nightshade house, divide it in two, keep one half, put the sisters in the other half with all their brass bedsteads, and be awarded a sackful of money by our grateful government. Frank said drily that we would have earned it. And though this was the last project on earth that we hankered after, we somehow didn't throw away the stack of expensively printed leaflets that were thrust upon us.

Even when we Got Away From It All one Sunday and drove at random into Kent, these invisible forces were hard at work pulling us sideways, landing us outside Sissinghurst Castle just as the gates opened. When the sightseers moved forward, so did we. It is probable that no other visitors taking pleasure from the gardens that day tried to equate Sissinghurst with their personal housing problems. But we found the whole layout so cosy and liveable and easy-looking, the vistas of distant blossom or casual statue or urn so deceptively simple, glimpsed between yew hedges or pleached limes or tumbling roses, that we came away dazzled, suffering from the early unrecognised symptoms of Sissinghurst-itis. I even suggested jovially to Frank on the way home that we should ask the Bristol agents to put us down for any small derelict castles on their lists.

Another tangent to our housing ideas was provided by Frank himself. I found him one evening with a pencil and drawing-block, trying out various house-plans, in which a natural bent for drawing and his experience over the mews, when the architects went bankrupt, gave him a head-start. When I asked him if he was thinking of building a house, maybe he caught some unintended overtone in my voice, because he laid the pencil aside and said that we might get that desperate but that it seemed rather hard work. I said it sounded fine except for who was going to supervise the work while Frank was in China and Peru. Frank said there was also the detail of finding a building plot, and he sat right down and sent off a pack of postcards asking the agents if they had any land to offer.

He had no replies whatsoever, but perhaps the cards acted as a catalytic agent, because, a day or so later, two quite interesting small houses were offered in the mail by Bristol agents, and the next day a few more, enough to make a second whirlwind car-trip to Bristol the following week-end worthwhile. We cheered up enormously and began thinking and talking of all the attractions of the Old City of Bristol, looking forward to seeing them again. Glancing backward, through the long blank tunnel of time that had passed since we ' bought ' the saucy little box on the hill, we were surprised to find that it had been only three weeks since that other trip. It was still mid-August, and anything could happen during the six weeks before moving day.

We left London Friday evening right after work, had dinner on the way, and about an hour short of Bristol and half an hour short of pub-closing time we shacked up at an old inn that was a great success. The drinks were generous, the natives friendly, the bed-sheets smelled faintly of lavender, and the night air was scented with new-mown hay. When I even found a stone hot water-bottle in the bed, on this balmy star-strewn August night, I declared, suggestible as always, that I'd like to live there forever. Frank didn't bother to propound the manifest disadvantages of such a step. Instead, he said he was asleep.

Next morning we woke early and refreshed, covered the distance to Bristol in jig time, and started house-hunting with a few curtain-raisers in which we had little hope. This lack of hope proved to be fully justified. For instance, ' The Old Farm ' wasn't so much old as just plain worn out, and after considering briefly the notion of living in the new cow-barn and keeping cows in the house, we moved on. As for ' Riverside ', which was down-wind of the local sludge plant, Frank said it should be called ' Sewerside '.

The fifth house on our list, sent to us on its own by an agent new to us, was our prime reason for coming west so fast. It sounded perfect in the blurb, and when we looked in through the curlicues of the Georgian iron gates, it was perfect. We saw an elegant little eighteenth-century stone façade flanking a pillared doorway, and set in a modest nicely kept garden. When we rang the bell, a pretty young woman came, smiling but puzzled, took the blurb from us, read it, and then fell about with laughing. Her well-bred shrieks brought her husband, and when he understood, he fell about too. They explained that our blurb was the very one the agent had given them two years ago before they bought the house. He had presumably merely neglected to remove it from his files when the house was sold. We asked the couple if there was any chance of their selling, and they giggled, " Not likely! " and wished us luck. We made a point of going straight to the agent to tell him of his gaffe, but he didn't seem abashed or even surprised. He had nothing else to offer.

Then we began a slow tour of all the agents who had written us and a few who had not. None had anything new. We both felt very low. So long as all the houses on our lists had stayed terrible, house-hunting had remained an impersonal, if somewhat unrewarding, routine. But now that we had had the misfortune to see exactly what we wanted, but belonging to someone else, it became an affair of the heart. As I said to Frank, as we drove away from yet another barren agent, our trouble was that our housing aims had risen too fast. Whereas previously our only yardstick for bliss had been our London mews, here we were suddenly hankering after a house built for people rather than horses, and what's more asking for it to be pretty to look at on the outside.

Frank cut into this melancholy talk by saying there was nothing wrong with our aims, they were fine, and he'd be glad to discuss them later, but right now, as soon as this ruddy traffic light changed, he wanted me to hop out and help him park the car in the one vacant space ahead, across the street from that big restaurant, where he suggested we have.a bang-up lunch before returning to London. So out I hopped and gestured him into the space, with the help of five or ten passers-by, all of us nearly driving Frank mad. And when we had collected our things, and locked the car, and turned round, what should be staring us in the face but a big shiny house agent's that we had never heard of!

Inside it was as good as outside. When we asked the flawlessly sculptured young blonde behind the desk why her firm wasn't listed in the classified phone book, she tossed us a warmly infectious smile and said they had been here so long that she guessed they supposed that every one knew them. When we told her we wanted to buy a small freehold house, that day if possible, her smile didn't slip an inch, she merely asked us, "Freehold or freehold and free?" Which was one up to her because we had to confess we didn't know the difference, and she explained very nicely that, in Bristol anyway, a freehold house might be on rented land, while with freehold and free, both house and land were unencumbered.

(It turned out that most of the houses we had seen were on rented land.)

From then on it was quite fun. Our snazzy young friend shared a big fat file with us, and after we had discarded all the houses we had seen (she had 'em all!) and all Deadly Nightshades and such, the file wasn't so fat any more. But there still remained two wonderfully freakish offers which we thought we owed it to our friends to inspect: a ' bijou Tudor dower-house ', quite near Frank's job; and a newly converted wing of somebody's old ancestral mansion, quite near in another direction.

As we went out of the door, we collided with a van-driver bringing in a large parcel. The blonde called to us to wait a minute and, slitting open the wrapping, she handed us a handsome stiff grey double-page auctioneer's leaflet bearing a glossy photograph of a house which, blow me down, was the one-size-bigger of the little eighteenth-century stone façade that we had mooned over that morning. The blonde said, " I don't know whether to show you this or not. It isn't at all what you want. But it is so pretty, and I know you like anything Georgian. The snag is that it isn't in tip-top condition, and it is a far far bigger thing than it looks here. There is an earlier wing behind, not showing in the picture, and there are masses of bedrooms and old outhouses and a vine and a giant mulberry tree and a couple of fig trees and so on. But no one has viewed it yet, and the auction isn't for another month. Why not go and see it? " We looked at the picture with

35

grudging admiration, such as one might grant to the Acropolis without actually wishing to own it, and said it wasn't quite our style. But she said to keep the brochure, and we did. So there went our slap-up lunch in the big restaurant. Instead we cadged a couple more cardboard sandwiches, this time from a milk bar, and set to work.

The dower-house had so much, but all in the wrong places. There were traces of a cloister in the chicken run; and the kitchen was sited in a tiny barrel-vaulted medieval chapel, where the bosses and gargoyles, high above, were swagged with boiler-pipes feeding the kitchen sink. The poky north-facing living-room was nothing. It and the stairs and the two stark bedrooms were so remorselessly overlaid by Queen Victoria's heavy hand that it would have taken an archaeologist and a fortune to free it.

We went off and sat on a broken column in the garden, and considered switching the kitchen with the living-room, and all it would entail, and the short time we were likely to be in Bristol, and whether, even if we achieved the impossible, we would really enjoy living in a medieval chapel with a lot of gargoyles. And we had to admit regretfully that it was too nutty a proposition for even us to undertake.

Our next port of call was at somebody's ancestral mansion, and the trouble there was that we had arrived too late. The jobbing builder who had bought it as a money-making venture had, in our opinion, gone hog-wild in converting the lovely old building to three separate dwellings, not only in splitting noble rooms into cubicles, bisecting fine cornices and ceilings, but also, even more senselessly, in nailing up and painting over the beautiful window-shutters, and tearing out old fireplaces to replace them with brick ones.

So that was that, and we were ready to call it a day. But as we were making our way toward the London road, we passed a sign, at right-angles to us, naming the village (something like Hucklebury) where the little blonde's Far Far Bigger house stood, and we decided to detour and take a gander at it.

The village, preceded by a few miles of rolling farmland etched with hedgerows and trees, was a dear little cluster of mellowed Cotswold stone, with a petrol pump, and a post office, and a few shops, and a square-set old church in a high-walled churchyard. And bang opposite the church, on the tiny village green, was instantly recognisable, behind wrought-iron gates, the big sister of the miniature classic Georgian façade which we had loved and lost that morning: the same stone gateposts, and the lacy ironwork of the gates, the same high stone protective garden walls, the same symmetrical two-storey house with the pedimented portico and the crowned chimneys. You had to look hard to be aware of the awkward bulk of the older back wing, tied on behind like the tail of a clumsy kite.

Closer inspection, when we opened the gates and walked up the short stretch to the front door, showed that both the house and the grounds beyond it were rather endearingly down at heel:

paint flecking off the windows and door, a few cracked panes, nettles in the front garden, a tangle beyond.

The front door stood open when we went to ring the bell. No one came and we rang again. The stone-flagged front hall struck agreeably cool as we stood on the step in the dappled sunshine. It was a large square hall, a trifle shabby, a bit overfurnished with pieces that were nothing special, adding up to a lived-in look. To the left and right were finely moulded closed doors, presumably to sitting-rooms, and at the back a pretty pillared arch opened to a graceful Georgian staircase. It was so quiet you could hear the bees in the garden. In the silence, the old clock tower across the road spilled an arpeggio and ponderously struck three o'clock. Then footsteps came running around the corner of the house, and a young man burst upon us. He was exceptionally handsome, and wore exceptionally grubby dungarees, which he apologised for, saying we had caught him up in the loft at the back, cleaning out the water tank. He said his mother and his sister were both out somewhere.

Spotting the leaflet in my hand, he said he hadn't seen the finished product yet, and read it over my shoulder. We all agreed that it was a stylish little document, and we explained the circumstances in which we had acquired it fresh off the press. At that, he drew an extra big breath and said that this was all very nice except that today mamma had decided not to sell the house after all! He explained that after his father's

38

death some little time ago, he and his sister had both felt that the upkeep of such a big house was too much for mamma, with both of them away most of the time, and she had agreed to having these leaflets printed. Then today she had a new plan: she would keep the house, live in the back wing, and let off the front wing. No, she hadn't told the house agent yet. The son said he would be very glad to take us round the front wing, to see if we might like to rent it, if we didn't mind taking things as we found them.

The room on the left was the dining-room, and on the right was the living-room, both largish well-proportioned rooms, well filled with heavy furniture and hung with heavy dark curtains on old brass rings, but with the delicately moulded window shutters still intact. The living-room fireplace had been replaced by a 'modern' contraption of mottled tiles, but in the dining-room (" five miles from the kitchen, and used only on fête days ", the son put it) the pretty grey marble original mantel still stood, but again blocked in by brown tiles. Back of the stairs were a small morning-room and a large coat-room, and from there a broad hall continued back inexorably through the old wing, which we didn't explore. Upstairs, left to right, were the main bedroom, two dressing-rooms, and a spare room, and at right-angles, another broad hall to the middle distance. I asked about such details as kitchen and bathroom, and he pulled a face and said that was the trouble. Both these details would be in mamma's half of the house. We didn't ask to see them. It occurred to us that, upstairs, a boxroom opening off the stairhall could be made into a bathroom, and that, directly below, the coat-room could be made into a kitchen. We asked the son if his mother would be prepared to make such alterations for us, and he said he didn't see how she could: it would be so costly.

At this we rather lost interest. After our experience with the London mews, we were learning to be a bit chary of investing in other people's property. Anyway, it was all too big, and too chancy, and too patently unrelated to any dreams we might harbour as to the ideal home. It was getting late, and we had to get started, and as we drove off we waved to the son, but we didn't even look back at Hucklebury House. We didn't even discuss it on the way home. We just enjoyed the luxury of not thinking about houses at all.

The Far Far Bigger Thing

I'm an optimist. In the last act of *La Bohème*
I'm still thinking that Mimi will pull round.

Len Deighton, *Billion Dollar Brain*

That Saturday night neither of us slept well.
I was for turning on all the lights and thrashing
through the whole housing problem, from The Old
Farm on. But Frank, who, if the Last Trump
happened to blow at three a.m., would say to
Gabriel: " Let's discuss it at breakfast ", turned
over and went back to sleep. So I thrashed alone.
At breakfast we found we had pursued different
avenues to arrive at the same astonishing terminus:

that we should make some kind of offer for Hucklebury House!

My reasoning, if you could call it that, was that the front wing by itself, even without plumbing and cooking devices, was as good a buy as the box on the hill, where we had planned to replace these services anyway. And that we could safely offer, for the front wing only, the same price as for the Box (*i.e.* half the price of the professor's house), to keep the ball rolling, without fear of having it accepted, while we caught our breath.

Frank agreed that the front wing was all we really wanted, and that it was as good a buy as the Box. The only sensible offer we had had was from the agents, for the whole house, and if we wanted to bid, that, in Frank's opinion, was to whom and for what we must bid. As to how much we should bid, he suggested that since we didn't particularly want the back wing and all that land, we should offer the same price as for the Box for the whole caboodle. If that horrified them, the next step might be to waive the ' two-acre field of rich pasture land at present let to a neighbouring farmer at £7 per annum ' (which I frankly hadn't even noticed) and let them auction it separately. I said drily that I could easily do without rich pasture land.

I was lost in admiration at Frank's brainwork, apparently accomplished while he was asleep. Accordingly, it being Sunday, with no one we could phone at the agent's office, we scribbled out, typed up and mailed two letters, one to the blonde, one to mamma, making a bid for the whole premises, subject of course to survey and contract and, alternatively, asking for first option on any new plan that mamma might have. We made it clear that we were interested only in buying, not in renting.

Then we went out for a spin in the car to blow Hucklebury out of our hair. We really did succeed for a while, except that I asked Frank what the heck we would do with the back wing if we had the bad luck to get it. He said we could presumably live in it while we did up the front wing, and then forget about it if we wanted to (he is a great forgetter), or if we felt energetic and were staying in Bristol long enough to make it worthwhile, we could always do up the back wing to sell separately or to let to a tenant, but that all this was a long way away. I said let's hope it stays that way.

The next thing that happened was that Monday morning, before Frank left for work, the blonde phoned to say that our letter had arrived and caused the phones to hum, as we had unintentionally beaten mamma to the gun in informing the agency that she had changed her mind about selling the house. What was more, the blonde added with great good humour, Frank and I had added to the confusion by making our offer ' subject to survey and contract ', a contingent offer not being allowable for a house committed to the auctioneer's hammer. If we wanted the house, she explained, we would have to make a flat offer, binding immediately. But she saw our problem, and was ready to advise mamma to hold the house for us for a clear two or three days, to let us get it surveyed, and to consult our solicitor. (That phrase again!) I caught Frank's eye and mouthed, " What about our offering price? " He repeated this to the blonde. " Oh, that seems fair to us," she tossed off airily, leaving me with the uneasy suspicion that we could have got it for less. As to a surveyor, Frank suggested the one we had used (or not used) before, and the blonde said yes, he was a good man, and she offered to phone him for us, which we accepted gratefully.

As to what in the world to do about a solicitor, Frank called his office to say he would be a bit late, and we got out the Bristol classified phone book (it was looking scuffed at the edges already), read down the columns, happily found a law firm almost next door to the surveyor and, for no other reason, chose it, and phoned it up. By fool's luck, this was the best thing we ever did. A voice answered the phone, identifying itself and apologising that his staff were not in yet. Even just as a voice, he instilled confidence, a thin old voice, remote and beautifully articulated, redolent of leather-bound law books, and perhaps just a thimbleful of vintage port. The part was a natural for Richard Goolden. He grasped the intricacies of our outlandish position readily and calmly, saying " hmmm " occasionally and asking a few pertinent questions, and said he would keep in touch with us after he had made contact with the estate agent, the surveyor and the solicitor for the other side. We put down the phone feeling that it was all too easy for words.

That evening he rang us back to say that the surveyor had just phoned, reporting that he had been out to see the house, that his survey was quite favourable, and that he would present a written précis the following day. The solicitor said he would phone us again when he had seen it. Things really were hotting up!

On Tuesday we had a spidery long-hand letter from mamma, enclosing, on loan, a 1934 blueprint of the house, which the son had shown us and we had asked for; and suggesting that if we still wished to buy the property as a whole, we might be willing to let her the back half. To this Frank replied that if we bought the house, we might eventually divide it; but that we felt we must start off by having the whole premises to ourselves, so that we could live and store furniture in the back part while the front was being done up and a new kitchen and bathroom fitted.

Tuesday evening the solicitor phoned to say that he had received the surveyor's report and was sending it on to us that night. He said it was a careful and explicit document, as he had impressed upon the surveyor that it must be, regardless of speed; and that he found two statements in it particularly useful: one, that the house for its age and character was in very fair condition (barring its decorative state and outside paintwork); and the other statement, stronger still, that there was, so far as one could detect, a marked absence of decay in the timbers of the house. He ended by saying that when we had read the report, we might safely instruct him to proceed.

On Wednesday (24th August) we bought the house! The surveyor's report arrived, and seemed all right to us, so we phoned the solicitor to go ahead. But if you think (as we did) that it was as simple as that, you are wrong. It involved a multiplicity of surprising steps.

It involved sending our solicitor a cheque for three hundred and fifty pounds. O.K., we expected that. The surprise lay in our solicitor saying he was holding onto the money, as a sort of umpire. I had the temerity to ask our solicitor (I was handling this step of the proceedings while Frank was at work) how the Other Side (a phrase I had caught from him) would know that he had this cheque stashed away. And he replied, with amused dignity, " Because I shall tell them so."

The next thing the solicitor had to know urgently, namely the exact date we wished to move into Hucklebury House, took a bit of figuring that evening. Frank was leaving the Air Force on Friday, 30th September. His terminal leave (to be spent in packing) took us to Friday, 14th October. So we set the 14th and 15th for moving out of the mews and moving in at Hucklebury. We relayed this to our solicitor, and he told us to be ready to post him the rest of the purchase price a few days before our possession date, say by 11th October, in order to clear it through the Bristol banks in good time.

So that was that. But for the solicitors it was merely the introductory pirouette in an elaborate tribal dance known as Preparing the Deeds.

Both sides were as busy as bees, buzzing away and making honey for us in the form of umpteen things to sign. One Sunday we dealt with two dozen documents and business letters, all directly concerned with procuring one house for two people.

Meantime we heard back from mamma. She took Frank's letter remarkably well, and agreed gracefully about the back wing, at the same time presenting us with a couple of new teasers. First of all, she hoped I might like to take on the daily woman who had been with her for twenty-one years, a suggestion meant, no doubt, in the most kindly spirit, but one that smacked so loudly to me of the time in Singapore when we took on a dear friend's dear old amah with calamitous results, that I drew in my horns, for the present anyway. Mamma's second suggestion, also a kindly thought, was that we might care to buy some of the household bits and pieces that she was getting rid of, and that we might like to come down, preferably at a week-end, to settle such details. Our enthusiasm for this idea was marred by the knowledge that over the past decade or so we too had been collecting bits and pieces. However, we replied suggesting we should go down by the early train on Saturday week, arrive at the house about eleven a.m. and stay about an hour, to look at the things she had for sale and to take some measurements. (*And*, we added to ourselves, to see for the first time the back half of the house we had bought!)

To this mamma dashed off a reply, that alas she wouldn't be there on Saturday week, and could we come Sunday morning instead? But that if it must be Saturday, she would ask her domestic help to let us in and answer questions. We wrote back that the Sunday trains didn't fit in, and that if the daily woman could be there on the Saturday morning, it would be fine.

Mamma followed this with a scribbled list of things she wanted to sell, saying she found it ' impossible ' to price them, but that if we would tick what we wanted, she would get them priced afterwards.

We had also heard from Tia, wanting to know the pH content of the garden soil. And when we didn't answer right away, she sent a postcard: ' What is garden soil? MUST KNOW.' This crossed mine to her, saying we would scoop her up a sample when we went down, and adding, as side-chat, that the owner wanted us to take on her daily woman and we were resisting. That brought a third note from Tia, showing an unexpected awareness of what went on *in*side a house, advising us to think twice before refusing domestic help as it was sometimes hard to come by in country districts. This would, she added, leave us more time for the garden.

I don't know just when it was that it hit both of us, like a revelation from on high, that we might be eligible for a government grant for dividing Hucklebury House into two separate dwellings. But it did hit us, and we scrabbled frantically around the mews and eventually turned up those expensively printed brochures that the man had pressed on us at that special housing exhibition in Oxford Street the month before. They were dandy pamphlets with the tiny exception that they didn't give any name, address, or phone number to apply to. So I spent a nice sunny morning huddled over the phone, trying various likely and unlikely government departments, until finally I came across a live wire who knew all about it, and he urged me to waste no time in getting onto the correct local authority for Hucklebury and putting our case to him. I said I wasn't sure whether we wanted to do anything yet, we just wanted information, and we might wait awhile, maybe a year, before deciding whether to divide off our back wing. At this he got terribly excited and said dear me no; if we were to do anything, we must do it now; that a grant, if given at all, would have to be given for the kitchen and bathroom we were installing in the front wing, since the back wing already had both; and that we would be entitled to it only if we applied before the work began.

So I spent the nice sunny afternoon phoning around in the Bristol area, and discovering that a whole Jacob's ladder of local authorities had jurisdiction over Hucklebury.

On the lowest rung was the Hucklebury Parish Council, which, as far as I could tell, consisted of one farmer in the village. When I told him we had bought a house in Hucklebury, he had some trouble in pinning down who I was and what I wanted. Finally a light dawned and he said, " Oh, you're talking about the Black house; owned by Mrs Black." I said patiently that it *had* been the Black house but now it was the Britton house. At which he baffled me even more by saying, " Oh, no, the Britton house is another house entirely." But when I asked him to elucidate, he just said that it didn't matter and to get on with it. When I asked him about the housing grant, he said this was the first he had heard of such a thing, and told me to get onto the District Council in the nearby market town.

They were the second rung of the ladder, and they quickly sent me up to the next rung, the Area Council in Bristol; who quickly sent me back to the District Council, to another chap who actually knew what I was talking about, and asked me to give him our address so he could send us the correct forms in triplicate, to be discussed at the next Council Meeting. But he promptly, and very pleasantly, disabused me of any idea that we might receive any such ' wild ' sum as the five hundred or one thousand pounds I had spoken of. He said the biggest grant he could recall was for fifteen pounds. So much for the expensively printed brochures! But when the triplicate forms whizzed in the next day, we decided to be devils and fill them in anyway.

On Saturday the 17th we took the early train to Bristol, and changed to a bus for Hucklebury. Or rather three buses, with free transfer tickets from one to another. What with the waits between buses and their leisurely pace in transit, Frank said he had never spent as long for four-pence. In the third bus, I told the clippy we had had to wait twenty minutes, in a queue, in a stiff breeze, and she said we were lucky because the bus came only once an hour. This presented a new personal problem for me, since I don't drive a car. I told Frank I had naïvely supposed that all English buses were as good as Singapore ones, where they come along every five or ten minutes.

The clippy put us down at the pub, and there it all was again, the toy village that we had never heard of a month ago: the petrol-pump and the post office, the clipped hedges and gay front gardens, the little shops and the church and the village green. And there was the house, so sweet and innocent, floating in the mild early autumn sunshine, as good as pie, as if nothing had happened to disturb its shabby, elegant equilibrium. As we opened the front gate, the clock struck eleven. We were on time.

Mamma's treasure (as we called the daily woman) met us at the door with her hat on foursquare and an expression to match, and though she didn't come right out and say so, she made it clear, wordlessly, during the first few minutes, that she found me a pretty poor substitute for mamma. But Frank, when he got me aside, said that she seemed quite harmless, and he suggested I should ask her to come and work for us for a trial period, several mornings a week, after we moved in. Which I did, mustering great cordiality. At this she said: " You'd *better* have me. All the girls work at the chocolate factory." Frank then asked her to direct him to the chemist shop as he wanted an aspirin. " Chemist shop! There's no chemist shop in Hucklebury." (Later we got aspirins at the post office.) That about finished our conversation with her.

Having none too much time, we took mamma's list of sale objects and romped through the house, losing ourselves and each other in the cavernous corridors at the back. Quite early on we ruled out, as being no better than those we owned already, most of the carpets and furniture, and all the linoleum, curtains and fittings. *En route* we discovered the bathroom, and later the kitchen.

The bathroom, two-thirds of the way along the back passage, was a true museum piece, with a huge bulbous antique electric geyser, overshading an old bathtub raised on claws. The loo was also in period. The hand-basin was new, with bright chromium taps.

From there we went on safari to look for the kitchen, which was on the floor below, down some dark back stairs. That kitchen was big enough to hold the whole District Council in plenary session, and its main features were a black Aga cooker and, a brisk walk away across the room, a wonderful old shallow stone sink (which we earmarked for the garden), and above it a cold-water tap, once brass maybe, and the tiniest possible early-model Ascot. On the floor were some foot-worn stone flags, which we also mentally consigned to the garden. In the credit column, Frank pointed out that the one power-plug in the kitchen was in a good position for our refrigerator.

Looking ahead, we thought what an inviting sitting-room the big kitchen would make, in some dim future, for a sealed-off separate cottage inhabited by total strangers. Next door was a fair-sized room, marked 'scullery' on the plan, where, behind a load of bric-à-brac, stood a pristine seventeenth-century spitted fireplace and Dutch bread-oven that no one had thought to mention. This room, with its window seat and leaded panes, would make a dinky little dining-room. And opposite it, the small 'garden-room' would convert to an excellent kitchen leading through the disused 'engine-room' to the stable-yard.

It was while we were out examining the vine-house and the motor-mower that we had our big scare of the day. We had taken the cross-path that divided the front garden from the huge overgrown vegetable patch, past apple and pear trees heavy with fruit, through the tumbledown vinehouse rich with sweet ripening grapes, and hence to the motor-mower, which Frank examined and said must be the prototype for the earliest model ever made.

It was when we turned back toward the house that we got the scare. For the first time, we saw the flank of the main house outlined against the sky. It was like the Queen Mary in harbour, viewed below from the dockside. Like some venerable fortress without frills. In the rear wing there were no architectural fripperies to disguise the fact that this was a very very big house. There was just an immense sweep of unbroken stone wall, towering dizzily up past the vast attics to the varying angles of slate roof, and above that the banks of crowned chimneys. The broad weedy driveway, turning the corner from the front façade, hugged the full length of the house, marching on and on beside it until it reached the roomy old stable, dwarfed in the distance.

It was all ours. We were committed. We were committed to the museum-piece bathroom, and the stone-flagged kitchen, and the rows of closed bedroom doors, and the garden walls and pigsties and stable and vinehouse, and the acre of garden, and the two acres of rich pastureland, and to that forbidding Queen Mary-in-harbour exterior. It was indeed a far far bigger thing that we did than we had ever done. Whether it was a better thing, remained to be seen.

Reasonable Creatures

So convenient it is to be a ' reasonable creature ',
since it enables one to find or make a reason for
everything one has a mind to do.

Benjamin Franklin

On the day after our lightning trip to Hucklebury,
we wrote to mamma, thanking her for giving us
access to the house, and noting, for the records,
that we had left on the hall table her list of objects
for sale, with check marks against the half-dozen
things that we wanted prices on. These were
mostly garden tools and such, but they included
an eighteenth-century black lacquer cabinet with

large cocks and hens in gold, silver and red, similar to one in the Victoria and Albert Museum, which was so pretty that it made me weak at the knees.

By now I was sorting things in the boxroom and tying labels onto all our furniture. (A visiting friend who found her chair labelled 'living-room' asked if we had to be reminded what room we were in.) Frank meantime was simmering up to quit the R.A.F. on Friday the 30th; and was leaving his packing until after then. He had notified Bristol that we were moving in at Hucklebury on 15th October, and that he could start work two days later. But when his new boss heard this, he nobly forbade Frank to set foot in the office until the 31st, giving us a welcome fortnight to settle in. We had three estimates from removers, and had nailed one for the 14th and 15th. We had sent off a pack of postcards to builders, electricians and heating engineers (culled —where else?—from the Bristol classified phone book), and of course had received no replies. In other words, everything was normal.

One thing that wasn't normal was the violent reaction our simple house-purchase had triggered off among friends whose pulse-rate hadn't accelerated throughout our previous twenty-odd moves. My sister in Boston was one of the few people who took it calmly. Inured over the years to our fidgety changes of habitat, she merely inquired in a postscript, ' How big is an acre? '—as usual hitting the nail on the head. Tia was another offhand one, as far as the house went. To her

56

the acquisition of a house was only a necessary adjunct to acquiring a garden. 'That miserable little envelope of earth you sent,' she wrote, after our trip to Hucklebury, 'is not very helpful in judging your soil. Next time dig deeper and send more, preferably from several places.'

With our other friends and relatives, what startled us was not so much the speed at which the word got around, which was about par, as how quickly fact ballooned into fiction. In no time our new house had taken on the dimensions of Buckingham Palace, we had a stableful of horses, and were breeding milch-cows. In one version there were peacocks on the lawn.

But the most interesting phenomenon was how emotional everybody got over us, and how people who had never expected logic from us before were suddenly seeking some deep screwy significance in our present move. In this they fell into three main groups.

The most vociferous group hauled back aghast and reiterated that we had gone out of our tiny pointed heads to undertake anything so totally out of character on this mad scale. They were the easiest to deal with. We just agreed with them and talked about something else. If they pursued it and asked why *why* WHY we had done it, not giving us a chance to tell them, Frank's usual reply was, " Why not? "

In the middle group, comprising our best friends, the main emotion was hilarity. They would get us to read out bits from the auctioneer's leaflet and then fall back helpless. (The rich pasture was always a show-stopper.) They had it figured out that we had bought the place because the village was called Hucklebury, and they were all for our getting embroiled in our project as fully and disastrously as possible so they could enjoy our discomfiture longer. With these two groups we were in perfect sympathy.

It was the third, small-minority, group, made up mostly of those who didn't know us very well, including the postman and milkman on their rounds, who made us really uneasy. We called them the Dream-Come-Truers. They were bent on endowing us with a whole raft of fancy compulsions, as if we heard voices, audible also to themselves, calling us back to The Land. They kept using embarrassing phrases like " Fresh air and exercise! " and " The simple life! " and " Digging your roots into the soil! " and, most eerie of all, " A place to end your days! " They were a little hurt when we snapped their heads off.

But in spite of such minor irritations, we were really enjoying life now that we had set in motion the main machinery of the move. Indeed once these things were settled, we had a week or so of false euphoria before the final push began. Pleasant little farewell cocktail and dinner parties sprang up all around, including our own champagne party in Claridge's Chinese room, which we enjoyed inordinately. Frank took in the Farnborough Air Show. We both made forays into the eighteenth-century rooms of the Victoria and Albert, and came home full to the brim of expensive ideas above our station. We haunted antique shops and even bought one or two pieces. Frank's mother contributed the family pie-crust table and three mid-eighteenth-century chairs to the cause, and Tia showered us with more eighteenth-century family furniture, which we had never had room for before. We went to receive a prize from our London borough for our small bomb-site garden (plants courtesy of Tia). And, with that accomplished, we rather guiltily dug up the rarest and best of her little shrubs and things to take with us, and were astonished to find that we totalled fifty pots, and still left behind a presentable garden for the next tenants.

Our last week at the mews was really a dilly. Everything happened. You know, like the prefab wardrobe we had ordered weeks before being lost by British Transport and Frank having to go and collect a replacement from a vast distance on top of a taxi, and then the original one turning up from Lord knows where. And the curtains not coming back from the cleaners, and our putting a firecracker under the cleaners, and then their sending us somebody else's curtains. Things like that.

And we had a letter from mamma, saying she hoped it was all right that the local amateur dramatic group were storing their scenery and props in ' my old engine room '. And we wrote back the same day, saying we were sorry, but it was not all right; that we should need all the space in the back of the house while the front wing was being done up. Three days before our move, she wrote that she had completed her move, temporarily into a friend's cottage, and that she would do something about the scenery and props.

Oh, and a few days before the move, I had a letter from the agent for my book saying simply, ' The lack of a good title is holding up production ', the first we'd heard of this. At a party we picked everybody's brains and drummed up about a dozen of what we thought were screamingly funny titles and sent them along. Next day the nice publisher phoned direct to say that the new titles were great fun but they didn't quite conform to their normal list of titles. So I looked up their normal titles to seek inspiration, found that they all ran something like *A History of Palæontology* and *The Doings of the Fifteenth Infantry Brigade,* and marvelled more than ever at their wanting my style of book. Finally I phoned the publisher back to ask if *he* had any ideas, and he said he'd have a think.

It was fixed beforehand that the movers would come early Friday morning the 14th, pack and stack things like mad until lunchtime, leave for Bristol right after, park the van in their Bristol depot overnight, and meet us at the house early Saturday to offload. And oddly enough, that is just what happened. Exactly at two o'clock, we and the van left the mews, with no regrets, and for a while we kept passing each other, waving cordially, until we broke away and lost them. I don't know where they slept, but we dossed down in such a cosily heated three-star hotel outside Bristol that we were amazed to wake in the morning to the first white frost of the season. We reached Hucklebury in unison with the movers at eight a.m., and when I produced our very own door key, sent us by our solicitor, and we flung open the big front door, it was quite a little ceremony. " I really feel that the house is ours," I said ecstatically to Frank. He quoted this back to me later.

Bearing in mind that we were leaving the front wing empty for the builders, the mover's foreman, who had obviously done his homework on the marked house-plan we had given him, sent his men in the van on around the driveway to the stableyard, while Frank and I sprinted through the house to unlock the stableyard door, the foreman sprinting along with us at a tangent for a brief recce of the rooms we were using. He caught up with us in the stableyard, blowing slightly, and asked if we knew that the room marked ' old engine-room ' on the house-plan was full of stage scenery. Frank said he didn't actually *know* it, but that it didn't surprise him (which left the foreman scratching his head). On a sudden inspiration, Frank asked if this stuff could be put in the stable (the only shed with a rain-proof roof), and the foreman went off for another recce.

He was back in a trice, and asked if we knew (his favourite form of imparting disaster) that the stable was full of junk too. He had not greatly exaggerated. When we got out there, we found the stable so full that when we opened the big old doors, things burst out. We all set to shoving the debris around, and soon found that a loose outer layer, made up of the elderly garden tools we had bought from mamma, was piled against three or four trunks marked with her name, which we hadn't known about.

Meantime another stout Cortez in the team came running with the news that the ' old scullery ' (the room with the spitted fireplace, which we had earmarked as our temporary sitting-dining-room) was chuck-full of junk (possibly waiting for the dustmen?), and he wanted to know where they should now put that furniture. So we took a deep breath and told the foreman to put our living-room furniture in the small morning-room up front, and our little drop-leaf dining-room table and its four chairs in the big kitchen. Now at last the men could start offloading. One of them asked where we wanted the refrigerator. We showed him, it fitted fine, and we all looked rather surprised when the inside light came on and the motor hummed. While I was stocking it with the cartons of food we had brought in the car, Frank went upstairs to switch on the bathroom water-heater. One of the men found some sticks and coal in a shed outside and lit the old Aga. It gave off a smoky warmth, combating the icy chill of the house. He produced a blackened tea-kettle from somewhere and put it on the hob for tea, that first essential of the working man. (Half an hour later he came to tell me that the kettle hadn't boiled yet, and I extracted our electric kettle from a box, and he reported proudly that he had plugged it into a wall-plug in one of the front rooms and it had boiled in three minutes.)

Meantime Frank came back and reported that turning on the water-heater upstairs was a major operation, not to be undertaken lightly; that for some reason it was governed from the hallway outside the bathroom by a giant lever, on the lines of a railway shunting lever, that he didn't think I would be able to budge. I said that was O.K. with me, as I had no intention of ever turning off any heat-making apparatus in this house.

Frank then opened the refrigerator to admire it, and asked why I had turned it off. I said I hadn't, but sure enough the inside light was off and the motor had stopped. He and a couple of the men fooled around with the switch-box, baffled, and then followed the flex as it ran, perfectly visibly, along the wall, out the door, and up the stairs, until I called up to him that the fridge was on again. Just then it went off again, and I relayed that. Then on again, and Frank reappeared grinning ruefully and said they had spotted the trouble: that both the kitchen wall-plug and bathroom water-heater were fed from the hall lever upstairs in such a way that you could use one or the other but not both at the same time. I said that for the moment I unhesitatingly chose the refrigerator. Frank said *he* unhesitatingly chose to have them both on, and that as soon as the movers had finished, he was going out in the car to look for an electrician. He said that right now he was going up to wash his hands.

In an odd tone of voice he then called me up to the bathroom. You remember that nice new hand-basin with the shiny chromium taps I told you about? Well, there were no water-pipes attached to them. There was an out-pipe under the drain-hole all right, so if you filled the basin, the water wouldn't just pour onto the floor afterward. But how to fill the basin with water? With a bucket? Or scoop it from the bath with your hands? Not a bit of it. Frank, that clever engineer, had it all figured out. You grabbed hold of the extra-long spout attached to the water-heater overhanging the bath, gave it a colossal tug, and made it swivel in a big circle around the room, leaking furiously throughout, until it came to rest over the hand-basin. Then you went back to the bath, turned on the tap with a wheel thing, and started turning it off immediately so it wouldn't overflow the basin. The word got around among the movers, who were just finishing work, and they all crowded in and wanted to try it. I told Frank it was sure to be a focal point at parties.

The foreman carried us off for a royal tour of the rooms they had furnished, and amid mutual expressions of esteem, we waved them off the premises. Then Frank went to look for an electrician.

In no time at all he was back, in convoy with an electrician's van, from which emerged a nice serious little man with a bag of tools, who didn't waste time jeering at our electrical set-up, he just got to work putting it right. He flew back and forth like a small nesting bird between the fuse-boxes under the front stairs and the kitchen and bathroom, and before we knew it we had neat on-off switches for the refrigerator and the water-

64

heater, and the shunting lever was ready for the junk-heap. It was wonderful. As Frank said, now if we wanted to, we could have an iced drink while taking a hot bath, like anybody else.

While the electrician was at it, I asked him if he could rig up another power-line to the kitchen to connect up the kinky new electric cooker which we had brought down from London in its virgin wrappings. But he winced as if I had bruised him physically, said the fuse-boxes were old-fashioned and already overloaded, and advised us to get on with rewiring the whole house. We asked him if he would care to estimate for doing it, but he backed off and said he didn't have the men or the time for such a big job.

After seeing him off from the front doorstep, we wandered back through the empty front wing of the house, where we hadn't had time to pause before. It was silent, empty, and beautiful. Released from the furniture that had cluttered it, it took on its own dignity and meaning. The rooms were the perfect size and shape. The doors and windows were just right. In the stone-flagged hall, the light archway resting on fluted pilasters introduced just the right element of Georgian frivolity. In the living-room (which was to be our dining-room), the black lacquer cabinet we were buying stood in solitary grace, as charming as we remembered it. I rubbed it with the duster in my pocket, and its soft colours responded and glowed, and a silver pavilion came into view. We stepped back to admire it. Frank moved forward and straightened the cabinet slightly, and two legs fell off. I said testily, for it had been a long hard day, that in this household one loose leg was to be expected, but two seemed excessive.

We went up to the bedroom we had chosen (the room above the kitchen and opposite the bathroom). It was remarkably cold. We switched on the silly little electric fire which had been an abundantly adequate extra to the central heating at the mews. Here it made not the slightest impression on the accumulated chill. We shut the shutters and lit the bed-lamps, unpacked sheets and blankets and made the bed, laid out towels, found hot water-bottles and took them to the kitchen to fill. In the kitchen, the old Aga was still alive in a listless way, but the kettle that the movers had put on to heat all those hours ago still hadn't come to the boil. It was also apparent that the kettle leaked ever so slightly; it produced a small rhythmic spitting noise, which was vaguely comforting, like the faint heart-beat of an invalid. Frank lifted one of the Aga's stove-lids to poke around, and an angry gust of black soot filled the air and settled on us. Frank thought the trouble might lie in the quality of the coal; we had paid for a ton, but it seemed to be mostly slack. He said that on the morrow we might sift through the fuel in the shed and throw away the dust; that in the coal shed there was a broken coal sieve. I said wouldn't it be nice if we could return all this broken equipment to R.A.F. stores in return for a new issue. Frank allowed that there was something to be said for the privileges of an R.A.F. quarter. He thought that on Monday we might go into Bristol and buy a few things, including a small Calor-gas cooker to augment the frailties of the Aga, until we could get an electrician to rewire the house and rig up our proper cooker.

I told him he was nice. He asked if I'd like to go back to the previous night's hotel for dinner. I told him he was nicer still, and I began to perk up, especially when he had assembled the makings of a dry martini. We adjourned to the morning-room for our drinks. It was a pleasant jumble of tightly fitted familiar furniture interspersed with boxes of books. The new thermostatic radiator which we had switched on earlier had been doing its stuff, and when we came in from the icy hall, we were met with a lovely fug. I asked Frank if it was all right to sit in a morning-room in the evening, and he said it was all right with him.

As we raised our glasses, the front doorbell rang, a loud jangle that echoed through the empty halls. We started as guiltily as if we were doing something illicit. It turned out to be a boy delivering a telegram. A London couple, the wife a Bathonian by birth, had sent us the message, ' WELCOME TO THE WEST COUNTRY '. To my shame, I burst into tears.

Jolly Sort of Lodgings

Here am I with a liking for what's wentersome
... and a wish to come out strong under circumstances as would keep other men down. . . . Jolly
sort of lodgings. . . . The rain's come through
the roof. . . . Popilated by lots of wampires, no
doubt. . . . My spirits is getting up again.

Dickens, *Martin Chuzzlewit* (1843)

When we had been in the house a week, I asked
Frank whether this had been our most harrowing
move so far, or whether time had drawn a merciful
veil over the other times. He said he wasn't sure,
but that the important thing was that this move
was over.

By now we were crazy about the house. Well, I had to confess that my happiest moments were when I was *not* in the old kitchen, or, for that matter, the bathroom, or any of the long glacial corridors that separated our two oases: the morning-room and the bedroom. Mamma's treasure was pretty critical of me because I wouldn't let her open the windows in these two rooms to dislodge the thick fug we had built up there. Sometimes when she didn't think I was looking, she would tiptoe in and up would go all the windows. But a sixth sense, otherwise known as a draught, quickly warned me that she was at it again, and I would race in and shut the windows.

We had never lived in such a big house. After the mews it was huge. Before breakfast every morning, Frank would take a stroll all the way to the front door to collect the newspaper and mail, and we hardly ever got up to the front wing after that, either of us, we were so busy. We had accomplished quite a lot in those seven days.

On Sunday we cleaned out the coal shed. We sifted through and discarded about three pailsful of coal dust for every pail of honest coal that we saved, throwing our discards onto a junk-heap of old tin cans that we found back of the stable. Then we cleaned out a pile-up of soot, ashes and clinkers from the various passages of the old Aga, and when we relit it and fed it the new high-calorie diet, it responded by singing a doleful little tune, which we took to be its version of coming to the boil, though the oven still didn't rise much above blood temperature, and we hadn't yet persuaded a kettle to boil on the top.

On Monday at nine (well, notionally at nine) mamma's treasure arrived for her first morning's work. I was prepared to make a small occasion out of this, and had laid out an extra coffee cup. But it was not to be. She appeared in the doorway like an avenging angel and, without preamble, cried, "What have you done with my small coal?" Frank lowered his newpaper (we were finishing breakfast in the kitchen) and said pleasantly that if she meant the coal dust, we had sifted it out and thrown it away. She said, "You shouldn't of done that," turned on her heel, and left the house, perhaps forever, we thought.

However, when we had finished washing the breakfast dishes, we went out and came across her at the junk heap, shovelling like mad. When we asked her what she was doing, she said, "Saving my small coal, of course. If you don't want it, I do. It might rain." From time to time, Frank went to take a peek, and reported that after she had shovelled the coal dust into sacks, she stored them in a derelict pigsty. When it came time for her to go home, she slung two sacks over her bike like saddlebags, and off she went.

On Monday too we phoned the Aga people, to ask them to come and apply a little first-aid, but when they had identified our Aga, they said they had been out some time previously, and had reported then that the best remedy would be a new one.

We had also gone into Bristol on Monday and

had come home with a caravan-size Calor-gas cooker as a stand-by, and a more efficient electric heater for the bedroom. Monday afternoon we had wandered over to the village shop and met the proprietor, whom we likened to Mr Grits the Grocer, in the card game Happy Families, because of his kindly smile. We started to tell him who we were, but he cut us off with a friendly gesture and said, " Oh, we know all about you! " which gave us food for thought.

On Tuesday, to our immense pleasure, a man from the county advisory service responded to our phone call and came to look over our garden with us. He tested the soil and reported on it favourably (just the alkaline side of neutral, we told Tia), and found the trees to be of interesting varieties, most of them dating from the turn of the century or much earlier, and healthy and flourishing " in spite of the weeds ". With one exception. He asked whether we were particularly devoted to the pair of giant beech trees in the middle of the lawn. He said they were suffering from some disease, and, being very shallow-rooted, might fall on the house during a storm. He added that while the trees remained, we would never have a good lawn. Frank asked who could fell them for us, and the adviser replied, " Ah, that's the problem." He said he couldn't recommend a firm.

After Tuesday the days tended to blur agreeably together. During that week the drama group (a nice bunch of youngsters) came to collect their scenery, with no initiative from us, and handed in a door key to our house. Frank said to me afterwards that this was only a minor factor in his wish to change at least some of the house locks right away without waiting for the builders. He said that our nightly business of locking up the house was getting to resemble the Ceremony of the Keys at the Tower of London. He had counted up that there were six outside doors to the house, each with a different key, only two of them (the front and back doors) with any spares, most of them too big to put in your pocket, and all of the locks of such rudimentary design that a burglar could open them with a hairpin. The conversation then deteriorated into a discussion as to whether burglars carried hairpins, Frank maintaining that the burglar he was thinking of had his wife along. But that was how it happened that our first positive step in renovating the house was to summon a locksmith that very afternoon to put identical new Yale locks on the two main front and back doors. We hadn't had a chance to warn mamma's treasure about this. Inevitably, when she arrived next morning, though we had remembered to have the back door propped open welcomingly for her, she marched into the morning-room where we were holed up and said " What have you done to my lock? "

We had also, that week, been busy ushering a stream of builders, electricians and heating engineers on conducted tours around the front wing. Of these, two builders, two engineers and one electrician *said* they had the time and the men and the inclination to submit estimates, but so far only the two engineers had buckled down and delivered to us their plans and costings for supplying oil-burning heat and hot water to the front wing. Of these two, the second was a hundred pounds cheaper than the first, and Frank liked his approach better. What I liked was that he *said* he could start on November first and that *maybe* he could finish in a month if he could get radiators and so on. " In for Christmas! " was his war-cry, which we privately modified to " in for New Year's " under our breath, knocking on wood.

The electrician, not to be outdone, said he could start November first too. All the builders we had met so far were less suggestible, and far less merry. I asked Frank if he thought the mere fact of being builders had contributed to their jaundiced viewpoint. Frank said that whatever the cause, it was indisputable that they were not very jolly chaps. We heard one of them muttering away, asking Providence to give him a nice new modern house where you could use a T-square on the carpentry. The other builder, on first entering our future living-room, pointed to a shallow bulge in the ceiling over the fireplace and suggested that it was caused either by subsidence or death-watch beetle. When we showed signs of acute alarm, he ripped up a floorboard in both the living-room and our big bedroom above (which he didn't deign to replace), and comforted us by saying that we should thank our stars that it wasn't subsidence, it was only beetles. I sputtered

that our surveyor had clearly stated that the
timbers of the house were markedly sound, at
which the builder chuckled ghoulishly (the first
time that he had even smiled after passing our
threshold) and replied, " Well, you'll have to sue
the surveyor then, won't you? "

I repeated this to our solicitor as a good joke,
next time we were phoning him, and to my
distress, his usual urbane good humour didn't
respond. Instead he replied soberly, " You may
indeed have to sue," and asked us to keep him
in the picture. We were flabbergasted.

Also that week, we had actually done some
gardening, if you could call it that. So far it was
mostly a blitz on nettles. In one great bed Frank
found a hedgehog all bundled up for the winter,
and after calling me over to admire it, he tucked
some nettles around it and told it to go back to
sleep. But by next morning it had gone. Frank
said it must have wakened in the night and felt
unhappy and wandered off to more congenial
surroundings. And darned if I didn't do the
same thing to the same or another hedgehog in
another bed the next day. Frank said that if this
continued, the hedgehogs would demonstrate.

That evening Frank told me that when he and
his brothers were children they used to put out a
saucer of milk at nights for the hedgehogs. I was
enthusiastic about this idea, and we put out a
saucer that very same night. But next morning
we found the saucer untouched except for one
huge muddy paw-print, belonging to some animal,
real or supernatural, built on the lines of the

Hound of the Baskervilles. So I didn't try that again. But we managed to finish weeding the two biggest nettle-beds without disrupting any more hedgehogs.

I wish I could report a similar degree of progress inside the house. In there the few rooms we were using seemed to get worse rather than better. I had a certain sympathy for mamma's treasure, trying to continue the methods she had used successfully for twenty-one years under the new conditions we were presenting her with. But, let's face it, under these new conditions she was quite a raiser of dust. Give her fifteen minutes in a room and a sirocco might have hit it. She was also blessed with exceptionally acute hearing. Frank, in the morning-room, would remark quietly that we might ask the treasure to start polishing the brass door-knobs today, and in a trice she would be looming in at the door, crying, "Door-knobs! We don't ever polish the door-knobs." If I were to remark timorously that they did look somewhat bronzed, she would close the subject by saying, " WE like them that way."

But what amazed us about life just then was, not how hard we were working, which we expected, but what fun we were having. It really was a joy-ride. We had such good little expeditions sandwiched in between slices of drudgery. One day to Bath, another to Wells, to visit antique shops, another day to Cirencester, to chase up a dealer we heard of who salvaged chimney-pieces from Georgian houses. (We wanted eventually to replace the junky early-twentieth-century fire-

75

place in what was going to be our dining-room.)

We had also discovered some more good country hotels to eat in. And the whole countryside was dotted with the most delectable stately homes, which we mooned over from the outside and made a note to visit inside at our leisure, when we *had* some leisure. Frank found it very amusing that on those days when we had paused to admire the great proscenium of, say, Badminton House or Longleat or Dyrham Park, when we arrived home and drove in at our own lacy iron gateway, I would catch my breath at the simple beauty of our own front façade, and tell Frank that I hadn't seen another place all day that I would rather live in than this.

The Men in my Life

> Work consists of whatever a body is *obliged* to do, and Play consists of whatever a body is not obliged to do.
>
> Mark Twain, *The Adventures of Tom Sawyer*

The day after Frank began his new job two lots of workmen arrived at the house to start tearing it apart: two electricians to rewire the place, front and back wings, and two heating/hot-water engineers to run a network of pipes through the front wing. We thus doubly ensured that no room throughout our quite sizeable house would at any time be deprived of falling plaster, floor-boards up, and little gnomes thinking up some highly technical question which they must have been confident I couldn't answer, let alone solve, before they asked it. For the first few days I covered sheets of paper, writing everything down parrot-fashion to ask Frank about when he came home for a peaceful evening. But I soon became so numbed or hardened that I would just answer the workmen with a " yes " or " no " as the mood took me, and hope for the best.

A third lot of workmen, the builder's gnomes, were supposed to be on hand when the other two lots started, to work ahead of them in cutting holes and taking up floor-boards. For instance, the builder's first job was to have been to cut a trap-door in the ceiling of the upper front hall, to give access to the front attics, which no one had set foot in for a century and a half. Since our interviews, a couple of weeks before, with the two reluctant builders who had outlasted the other five starters, we had been carrying the winning thought that one or both of them would come thundering down the straight at the last minute and give us their estimates, but fate willed otherwise.

On the previous Friday, when the mail hadn't brought anything from either builder, Frank phoned them both. The first one, sounding more discouraged than ever, withdrew from the field right then, confessing that the pressures of life were too great for him even without our job intruding into his worries. The other builder was more hopeful (if that isn't too cheerful a word).

He and Frank had quite an amicable little conversation in which Frank *thought* he said that he would get his estimate to us over the week-end and would stand by to start work on Tuesday the first.

When Monday came, with still no word from this second builder, Frank suggested, as he left for the office, that I should phone the chap and jog him up a bit. Which I did, with disastrous results. The builder said he was cut to the quick by my tone. He said he had had a perfectly delightful conversation on Friday with my good husband in which not a discordant word was said about any need for haste; that the trouble with us ladies was that we expected everything to be finished yesterday; and that he knew what he was talking about as he was a married man himself. To my horror I heard myself saying right out loud, " Your poor wife! " That was the end of *that* builder as far as we were concerned.

In the course of the morning Frank phoned in, and I asked him if he'd care to have another perfectly delightful conversation with our sensitive friend, to smooth down his feathers, and Frank said he most emphatically would not; that he was not going to waste time urging some builder chappie to accept several thousand quid from us if he didn't want it. He suggested I should ring the engineer and electrician, explain our predicament to them, and ask if we could count on their starting tomorrow without benefit of a builder. So I did, and they both said they didn't care a hoot whether a builder came or not. In fact the

engineer gave me the name of a builder we hadn't
tried, and I phoned him, and he came haring out
to make a spot estimate which was considerably
cheaper than the other two had guessed, and he
said he would write us up his specifications within
the week, and be ready to start work in a fortnight.
He was still there when Frank got home from work
that evening, and they seemed to take to each
other. But when I mentioned this to Frank, he
said he would take to the devil himself if he was
willing to get a move on.

Tuesday morning early the two engineers arrived and they were the nicest lads I have ever
gone through hell with. Having no builder on
tap didn't depress them at all. They just borrowed
Frank's saw and hacked a hole in the ceiling and
climbed up Tarzan-fashion, easing themselves
between the jagged edges of plaster and lathing into
the darkness above. Then they called down to me,
and I came running, to ask if I had an inspection
lamp. I said I didn't, but that to start things
off I would lend them one of our alabaster bedside
lamps, and when that turned out to have not long
enough a flex, I brought one of the silver candle-
sticks from the dining-room table. (Later on I
learned more caution.)

I felt so involved in their project that I waited
in the hall below, with plaster gently sifting onto
my hair, while they gave me a running commen-
tary. I even climbed to the top of our kitchen-
steps to peer upward, by flickering candlelight,
into a huge high-vaulted windowless chamber
timbered with whole trees, like the inside of a

cathedral at night. The candlelight diminished as the boys picked their way along the joists into the gloom. Suddenly they burst into gales of mirth, and came back to explain the joke. They handed down the orderly little blueprint their boss had given them to work from, in which neat dotted lines represented the pipes which were to circulate along the attic floor on a geometric course, dropping outlets into the various rooms below. Well, the joke of it was, they explained, choking with laughter, that the dotted lines didn't allow for a few obstacles such as great rough-hewn beams and massive angle-blocks, and, best of all, a good solid Cotswold stone partition wall, maybe two feet thick, floor to rooftop, which they had just run up against.

Undaunted, they came down and borrowed a crowbar from Frank's tools, bending it only slightly in prising enough boulders from the wall at waist-height to let them clamber through, taking the candlestick with them. This was followed by whoops of glee, and they came tumbling down through the hole to report that there was another stone partition wall for them to break through, a dozen feet or so beyond the first wall. Then there was a long sober silence, punctuated with a falling of rocks that shook the house, then shrieks of joy, and the larger of the two lads came racing down to report, his face grimed and his eyes dancing, that the smaller lad had lowered himself through the new hole into total darkness, to find that there was a four-foot drop in the floor level of the new section, so that he was now about six feet below the level of the hole and couldn't get back. So the big lad borrowed a rope from Frank's things and lassoed it to a beam, and the small lad climbed up it like a monkey. All in all, it was a bit of a comedown when the boys finished their cliff-hanging and reverted to the workaday routine of screwing together lengths of pipe in the stableyard, to the background singing of 'Davy Crockett'. Before lunch—in fact barely in time to lay off for lunch— the two electricians appeared, and joined in four-part singing that rocked the house.

The next day the engineers were joined by a third man whose sole function in life was to make little holes. He was a sweet old fellow with a rubber face and a continual vague smile. At one point he insinuated himself so silently into the big empty upstairs room where I had set up the electric sewing-machine and was creating my own noise, stitching curtains, that I got quite a start when I looked up and found him sitting on the floor cross-legged, scrabbling away. Feeling a certain social obligation toward him, I tried out my rather frayed charms by asking him whether he had a master plan as to where to make holes or whether he just put them where he felt like it. At this he rose abruptly to his feet and made for the door. "No, no, please continue," I cried, fearing I had offended him, but it turned out he had merely gone over to fetch a pair of steps which he, still wordlessly, climbed up and switched to making little holes in the ceiling. After that we just smiled at each other periodically, to observe the niceties. It was quite a while before I discovered that this dear little man was a deaf-mute. He had been with the firm for donkey's years and they all loved him and played little tricks on him which he adored.

About a week later, the builder arrived unheralded and in great haste, deposited one workman (a foreman named Les), and departed. Les, a tall spare man, with sinewy good looks, and a delightful vocabulary which he kept well-exercised in the course of duty, was for the moment a general with no army, and he told me that he would perceed with orientitting himself. He spent about an hour doing this, refreshing himself with frequent cups of tea which he delegated the heating lads to brew for him. The first phase of his orientitting was to examine the hole into the front attics which the engineers had hacked in his absence. This pained him terribly, and he looked at me resentfully as if I'd done it and said, " The cost of making this good will of course be extra to the estimate "—a phrase that in varying contexts became as much a part of his daily ritual as the tea break. In him the builder had a trusty chief of staff.

Meantime at week-ends Frank and I were making real headway in the garden, in spite of the discouraging announcement on the radio that this was the coldest November since 1947, which we didn't doubt, especially indoors. Frank had bought me three expensive presents, more welcome than jewels: a pair of fleece-lined Wellingtons, some fur-lined gardening gloves, and a ' ladies' size ' garden-fork and spade, the ones we had bought from mamma being so heavy I couldn't lift them off the ground. With a little practice I could now clear weeds, to the depth of one foot, from frozen ground, at top speed, just ahead of Frank, who levelled the ground with a light roller we had bought, and cut and laid grass turf from another part of the garden. This crazy project was an example of pure Sissinghurst-itis. We were, the dear Lord help us, in the process of creating a seven-foot-wide grassed avenue that Frank had dreamed up, twenty-five yards long, which until about day-before-yesterday had been waste ground, cabbage stumps and weeds, and which, if our health lasted, he was bent on edging with a hundred baby yew trees which he had already ordered. This would eventually, even if we weren't still here to admire it, lead the eye, Frank told me, through a medieval stone archway (which he was going to have some so-far-hypothetical stone-masons move for us from a part of the garden where it didn't show) and hence to a little orchard (no fruit-trees yet; it was now a disused tennis-court with tall grass to the armpits) carpeted with spring flowers (still to be ordered and planted). Beyond that, the eye would wander over our two acres of rich pasture where several of our farmer-tenant's cows were tastefully arranged.

We had already exchanged a few words with the farmer-tenant and wished we hadn't. He told us that some of the hedges in the field weren't stock-proof, and apparently expected us to do something about it. To take his mind off this, I asked him chattily if he had any land of his own. He replied tersely, " Yes, thirty acres." That took me down a peg or two. It wasn't quite the way I had envisaged the good old feudal landlord-tenant relationship.

About then, the tenant of one of the little cottages along the road, which backed onto us, hallooed at us over the garden wall and asked us when we were going to chop down the grove of trees that shielded us from him. He said they shaded his cottage. From the proficient zeal with which he threw himself into this discussion, it was apparent that he was hopefully continuing a long-standing skirmish.

From the third side of our walls we were approached in a grieved tone by a cottager who said the previous owner had promised to sell him a pie-shaped wedge out of our land to build a garage on, and how about it? We told him we weren't interested, right now anyway.

At this point, Frank came back from the office and mentioned casually as the evening wore on that there had been some idle talk today about his going on a tour of Australia, with stop-overs in South America. I asked him if he planned to direct operations here by remote control.

Around then, too, I had a letter from the publishers saying they suggested the title *East of the Sun* for my book, and they hoped we would approve. We did so, but Frank had me put it on record, in my reply, that Singapore wasn't really east of the sun; that the sun rose there in the east the same as any place else. The publishers thanked me with bland courtesy for reminding them.

At this juncture we were invited to our first cocktail party of the season, given by some local gentry in a lovely ye-olde-worlde house in the next village. So I scrubbed my hands and fingernails and unpacked a dressy dress and pressed it, and off we went. We weren't sure, talking it over afterwards, whether or not we had met any soul-mates (it's kind of hard to tell right off the bat). But everyone was charming and cultured and beautifully dressed, and, I might add, very nice and hospitable to us, practically straining a ligament trying to find some topic of conversation we might share. The host didn't lessen this task by introducing me around as a "lady authoress" (my least favourite form of tautology). During the horrified lull in general conversation that followed, I protested that it wasn't really like that; that like everybody else in the United Kingdom, I had written a book, but that mine wasn't even published yet. It turned out that our host was a friend of a friend of my publisher. One wonderful old lady came up in a state of alarm, drew me aside, and whispered, "Please don't put *me* in a book." I promised faithfully that I wouldn't. And here I go breaking that promise! Another senior citizen drifted up and asked me if I knew Ivy Compton-Burnett or Virginia Woolf, and when I said I didn't, she drifted off again.

Meantime Les the foreman was still coming in without his troops, and was still orientitting and drinking tea. After a bit, Frank cornered him and asked what was holding things up. " Bricks," Les replied cryptically. When prodded to elaborate, he said that we had specified hand-made bricks, and that if ordinary builders' bricks weren't good enough for us, we must wait for them. That was Friday afternoon late. So Frank phoned the builder, found that Les spoke the truth about the bricks holding things up, and found out from the builder how many bricks he needed. We then phoned the Bristol Building Centre, with whom we had become quite pally of late, and they gave us the name of a local factory that made hand-made bricks. We phoned this factory forthwith and asked them how soon they could supply the number of bricks we needed, and they said, " Tomorrow, or Monday if you want us to deliver them," but that we must come in tomorrow to choose the colour and pay for the order. So we did. And we phoned the builder and told him to have his full team at the house on Monday. And, amazingly, he did. The only snag was that on Monday both the heating engineers and electricians were called off on other jobs, so for a while we had only the builders.

On Tuesday two things happened: a woodworm man came to inspect, and I had my first formal caller. The woodworm man quoted such an astronomical figure for ridding us of death-watch beetle that he and I soon parted, never to meet again. Anyhow I had meantime consulted the Building Centre again, and they had put me onto a free advisory service called the Timber Development Association, who were going to come out in a few days.

My caller was the nicest thing that happened that day. She arrived in white gloves, exquisite clothes and a clean face, and caught me grubby from head to foot, in an old blue overall with the pockets bulging with dusters and screwdrivers. The engineers had taken up a wide row of flagstones right across our front hall, which they naturally left like that when they vamoosed, and the aplomb and ease with which my visitor vaulted that ditch, as if it were Becher's Brook, endeared her to me instantly. She settled into our scruffy little morning-room all bulging with furniture, tactfully refused tea and accepted a cigarette, paused for a brief amusing chat, and asked us to dinner a few evenings ahead. Then she vaulted the ditch again and was gone, leaving me quite unreasonably pleased with life.

I decided that part of my trouble lately had been that I never seemed to see any women, except mamma's treasure. It had of course always been my secret ambition to have quantities of men knocking at my door. But not these men. They didn't knock. They just opened and entered any room I happened to be in, and however they found me, they didn't seem to notice, which was perhaps just as well.

When December came and we had had men in the house for a month, I decided that another of our troubles was that never, in all our moves, had we been in such a state of concentrated havoc on such a big scale and for such a long time.

All three lots of men were now back on the job, but their only progress seemed to be in the degree of disintegration they had achieved. In every room floor-boards were perpetually up. The walls now had as many holes accidentally or intentionally knocked in them as an old piece of Gruyère cheese. The driveway was gashed with channels for new water pipes. And yesterday the tree man had arrived to fell the pair of huge ailing beech trees that shaded the lawn and endangered the house. We had found him (need I say?) in the Bristol classified phone book. He was young, strong and apple-cheeked, with such nice manners and such trustworthy limpid blue eyes that we quickly dispensed with a written record (which he declared to be not usual or necessary) of his agreement to come on that date, chop down both trees, saw them into portable lengths, remove them to a timber yard, and pay us ten or fifteen pounds according to their condition. Yesterday he had come at the right time, had felled one tree with a tremendous thud that echoed through the village, the felled tree and its twin shivering like wounded animals as the giant lay there sprawled over the whole garden; had cut it, as it lay, into six-foot lengths, loaded its main lower trunk and a few of its heavy branches onto his little vehicle, and whisked off, leaving us with great segments of tree-trunk and branches everywhere, and ugly scars all over the lawn from his tractor wheels.

Just then, with everything looking its best, a Canadian air marshal, who had been Frank's boss during a phase of the war and had been awfully nice to us both, phoned from London that he had just arrived in the country and was lunching with the Admiralty in Bath tomorrow, and could we give him a bed tomorrow night? We instantly said no, but heaven help him and us, we found ourselves asking him over in the afternoon and offering to take him out to dinner and find him a hotel room. To make things even gayer, the tree-felling man appeared without warning with two mates that same afternoon after several days' absence, and proceeded to fell the second tree, which meant that now twice the original area of lawn and flower-beds was cluttered with segments of tree-trunk and fountains of branches. Then they went away again, leaving the chaos to us. The air marshal had been all for shouting " Tim-bah! " to give some zest to the operation, but the tree men looked at us as if they thought we were all slightly bent, so we went inside again.

This, our first party, was quite a success. By now we had rigged a rickety bridge over the foss in the front hall, over which Frank led his present boss and his wife, to meet the air marshal for drinks in the morning-room. Then we took them all to dinner in Bath, at the Hole in the Wall, and afterwards dropped our friend at his hotel.

That same week, the timber adviser, who had been held up by 'flu, came to examine the place for death-watch beetle. Well, there's no account-ing for tastes, but as he crawled ecstatically around the floor, he seemed simply thrilled, both at the wonderful convenience of having floor-boards up in every room, but better still from his viewpoint, at the exciting evidence of death-watch that we could provide. And not only death-watch (*Xestobium rufovillosom*) either. We could also offer evidence of the common furniture beetle (*Anobium punctatum*). The only drawback to his present examination, he said, was that winter was the hibernation period for these lovable insects, so we must contain our impatience to see them until early spring. Even then we might be doomed to disappointment. We must steel ourselves for the possibility that all these numerous exit holes were old and disused, once tenanted by a happy breed of Georgian death-watch beetles which had thronged in when the house was new to feast on the delicious fresh sap. But if we were lucky, it might well be that there was still a live colony deep in the beams, and if so, when spring came they would shake off their sleep and come out to sun themselves on a window-sill or floor-board. He said if we saw even one live one (and he showed us its picture—a rather sturdy little beetle with cabriole legs), would we please post it to him immediately. " In a match-box? " I cried, carried away with enthusiasm. He regarded me chidingly, as if I were a backward student. " No, it could eat its way out of a matchbox, couldn't it? " he replied gently. He said a small tin or bottle would be best.

He was quite scornful of the woodworm ' expert ' who had been to see us, whose idea of the right treatment for death-watch was for us to have somebody else take up every third floorboard throughout the house every year for five years so he could spray some insecticide on the joists, and for us then to get somebody else back in to nail the floors down again. The timber adviser said this was worse than useless and would be an intolerable inconvenience to the householder. (This had actually occurred to us.) He said that in his view the only effective treatment for death-watch (and it would of course kill all other house-insects at the same time) was to carry out a complete fumigation of the whole house, using hydrogen cyanide at a high dosage for an exposure of seventy-two hours, with the house vacated for a week. He said there were only a few firms in England equipped for such an operation, and of these the London Fumigation Company, who had done a fine job on Nelson's ship, the *Victory*, had a branch office in Bristol. He left with us an armload of literature, describing the wealth of different insects a family could hope to rejoice in. Out of thirty-one possible pests, our favourites were the drug-store beetle, the red-legged ham beetle, the steam fly, and (as God is my witness) the confused flour beetle.

On the way out he buttonholed Les the foreman, who, teacup in hand, had been listening with us, and warned him that it was important at this stage to remove and burn any timbers that were so badly affected as to be no longer able to carry the load for which they were intended, and that new timbers should be painted with creosote. Les replied that anything like that would be extra to the estimate.

That same day we phoned both the London Fumigation Company and our solicitor. The solicitor expressed deep concern, and asked us to keep him posted. The fumigation company sent out a man the next day, who confirmed everything the timber adviser had said. In a few days he sent us an estimate, to keep by us in case any spring sun-worshippers emerged. This, while still big enough to make our hair curl, was over fifty pounds cheaper than that of the first 'expert', even excluding carpentry bills.

A week before Christmas (five working days to go) we paused to take stock. On the credit side, we didn't have just one Christmas tree like everybody else; we had a hundred baby yew trees (for our avenue) that had been laughingly delivered a month before we had asked, and it seemed easier to accept them and heel them in in a bunch than to make a fuss and return them as was our first inclination. But even in our frustration we had to admit they were cute little trees, each one a perfect Trafalgar Square Christmas tree as seen through the wrong end of a telescope. Quite aside from the fact that it was now snowing briskly, we couldn't plant them until the tree-feller came back and removed his tree-trunks and branches from the mangled remains of the grass avenue we had turfed so vigorously in November, and the tree man hadn't been seen for going on three weeks now. Les was also claiming that it was because of the tree man that he couldn't finish laying the outdoor polythene water-pipes, and that until they were laid there was no hurry about connecting the pretty pale blue enamel sink which lay propped in its wrappings against the wall of what was to be my dinky new kitchen, in the front cloakroom off what was to be our new dining-room if we lived that long.

The electrician took another view about the cause for *his* delays in connecting up the lovely new electric cooker we had brought down from London two whole months before. He said he couldn't possibly connect it before Christmas because Les had forgotten to order the glass bricks that were to make up the wall behind the sink. To prove his point, he took me into the new kitchen to show me how the snow was gusting in through the great six-foot-square hole Les had cut in the wall, and he said if he connected the cooker right beside that hole, it would cause a short in five minutes. So I called Les in and read him the riot act, and said I was going straight to the phone and see if I couldn't procure some glass bricks as quickly and readily as we had with the hand-made wall bricks earlier. But Les said with some satisfaction that it wouldn't help as the boss had taken the two masons off on a rush job until after Christmas. I asked him if he didn't consider *this* a rush job and he said he'd have to ask the boss about that.

All in all, somewhere along the line I had rather lost that initial childlike faith in the three lots of workmen who were cluttering our house, that is so desirable between employer and employee. When I asked for a report from the central-heating man, whom I caught drifting through that day, he stopped and focused on me, as if trying to remember who I was, and said airily that he was hoping for a completion date early in February. When I tactlessly reminded him that he had started out with a Christmas completion date, he said absently, " Did I? " and added that they were having trouble with radiator deliveries. Then he brightened up and reminded me that the builders hadn't finished the boiler chimney and hadn't put the oil tank in position yet. So, back to Les. *He* said they had run out of bricks for the chimney, and they couldn't put the oil tank in position until they had finished the chimney. Out of curiosity, I asked Les what *his* completion date was, and he said he didn't have one. So at least we knew where we were with the builders: nowhere.

Deprived of the big oven of the new cooker that I had counted on for the largish turkey I had ordered from MacFisheries, I went back to the old kitchen and measured the interior of the old Aga's little oven, phoned Mac's, told them to cancel my order, and asked if they had a turkey not more than six inches high and twelve inches square. " What weight do you want? " the manager asked. I said I didn't care what weight as long as it was that size. I could hear him repeat this to a minion, and then some hearty laughter. When he had controlled himself, he came back and said they didn't have one. So I went over to the village butcher, across the green from us. He thought my request was perfectly sane and reasonable, retired to the back room with my tape measure, and returned with a beautiful white capon of just the right size, which he offered to hang for me until I wanted it.

We now had only seven workmen milling around the house simultaneously, whereas I was used to nine. I sometimes wished that either they had a bigger repertoire of songs for part-singing or else didn't have any repertoire at all, or that their favourite tune wasn't ' Tea for Two ', because it gave me the urge to chime in with " Tea for Nine " on the choruses. They all tramped into the old kitchen for tea at 10.30, 12.30 and 3.30 on the dot. They made their own tea, but the kitchen looked a bit like a cattle yard when they were through, and it took nippy footwork on my part to toss together any meals for Frank and me in the intervals between tea hours. Still they all seemed awfully nice lads, if I could understand a word they said in their broad West Country accents. They couldn't understand a word I said in mine.

In spite of all this, Frank and I were having quite a bang out of life. (' Bang' was the operative word these days.) For instance, we had found and bought in Bath a D-end Georgian dining table with a square centre leaf, and, from the same shop, six really lovely Regency sabre-legged dining chairs (two with arms and four not). The shop-keeper said she would store them for us until we were ready, " until spring if need be ", perish the thought. So that was to be our Christmas present to each other.

One black snowy blowy evening, just before the holiday started, when the men had left for the night and I had locked up and was alone, waiting for Frank, the front doorbell rang with its great jangling sound, and I went and found the electrician on the doorstep.

He had been splicing cables in the stable, had got himself locked out of the house, and wanted to ask me some questions. As he droned through his usual interminable list of highly technical electrical problems which he expected me to solve on the spot, the snow blew in past his shoulders onto me and powdered the hallway. Finally I said testily, "Come inside so I can shut the door. And bring your mate in with you," I added, beckoning to the shadowy figure that had been lurking behind him in the dusk all this time. The electrician looked over his shoulder and said, "He ain't my mate." At that the shadowy figure stepped forward into the light and cried gaily, "*I* am the electrician's mate!" and I could see that his collar was on backwards. It was the vicar who had come to call. He was a delightful man. When Frank arrived he found us sharing sherry and nuts and discussing local history, on which the vicar was hot stuff.

On Christmas eve, the postman brought me an astonishing, pleasant and demoralising present: the page-proof for the Singapore book! I had had no idea that they had progressed so far. I was walking on air, and we started straight in proof-reading it; though actually there was little to correct, it was printed so accurately and elegantly. There were so few changes from my manuscript that one or two of my typing fumbles had slipped into print. Aside from that, they had left in Americanisms like 'gabfest', but had changed 'elevator' to 'lift', and had elevated (or lifted?) some of my American spelling to Queen's English.

It was especially fun having this arrive on Christmas eve, because afterwards, when I got down to the proof-reading more seriously, it was all tangled in my mind with our peeling and squashing chestnuts to stuff the capon, and with trimming the baby Christmas tree we had bought, and with hurdling Becher's Brook to applaud a remarkably large number of village carol groups, some children, some adults. The most amusing of these were three spirited infants, maybe six or eight years old, who couldn't sing for toffee but had bags of personality, and who were so overcome by Frank's giving them sixpence and cookies that they kept coming back for repeat performances. Each time they were clearly recognisable to us, not only by their distinctive style of singing, but by their impish leader's spectacles, tied together with string.

On a clear starry night just before Christmas, when it was so cold outdoors that the ice tinkled on the branches and squeaked and crackled underfoot, we were summoned to the front door for the third or fourth time that evening, expecting, perhaps, one more farewell performance from our winsome trio. Instead, there stood in a tiny semi-circle facing us, a larger group, of seven or eight assorted children, teenagers down to tinies, the contours of their rosy cheeks picked out be-witchingly in the up-light from several oil lanterns which they had placed on the ground before them. In each mittened fist was clutched a handbell, on which they proceeded, with remarkable skill and panache, to play a series of Christmas carols. After wild applause from us, they played them all a second time, capping the lot with ' Pop Goes the Weasel ', and they said that that exhausted their repertoire. Over cakes and soft drinks in our chilly bisected front hall, they told us that most of them belonged to one family, named Angel, from a farm just up the road which we had often admired. And Frank told them that this was the first time we had ever entertained Angels unawares.

When they left, they promised to come back next year and play inside the house to our guests at the best Christmas party we could manage to produce.

The Hazards of the Countryside

I had the symptoms, beyond all mistake, the chief among them being 'a general disinclination to work of any kind'.

Jerome K. Jerome, *Three Men in a Boat*

A few days after Christmas, the tree man at last returned with a couple of helpers to continue clearing away the great solid hunks of splaying branches that had been spread-eagled over our garden and driveway since the day, a month before, when we had, with such light hearts, watched him start to fell the pair of giant beech trees in the middle of our lawn. All morning the three men worked, sawing and chopping and heaping their little tractor with back-breaking sections of timber, and trundling it back and forth to dump the loads somewhere unknown, without, seemingly, making the slightest dent in the total of timber and debris still embedded in our wintry ground.

It was around noon that I smelled the smoke. When I went to a side door to look out, great clouds of smoke and live sparks met me. It was a horrifying scene. The tree men were deliberately drenching the branches with paraffin and setting them alight! Even the lawn was ablaze. Not bothering with a coat, I ran out hell for leather, shouting at the top of my voice for the men to stop. At the moment when I caught their full attention, and they all three turned to me in surprise, and several of our own men had stopped work to poke their heads out of upstairs windows, a square of rotting boards in the middle of a flagged path (which Frank and I had wondered about several times) gave way under me, and I fell down a well. As I fell, just like Alice, I could hear pebbles that I had dislodged splashing far below. But (unlike Alice) when *I* got to the hip-line in my little well, I stuck fast and could move neither up nor down. As the men grasped the situation, I could see their faces change from alarm to pure delight. Not one of them raised a finger to help me as I tugged at the sides of the well for purchase, clambered out, dusted myself off, and tested myself for bruises. Then, like a baited bear, I turned on the audience who were jostling each other for places at the windows, and I called out in exasperation, " All right, boys. The show is over. Now come and help me put out the fires that these silly clots have started."

And they did. They poured out of the house, bearing any receptacle they could snatch up, formed a bucket brigade, and set to extinguishing the myriad flames. There was only one group of men who didn't help: the tree men. They were busy collecting their belongings and departing. I called after them, but they didn't seem to hear me.

This left us with a serious situation, quite aside from the situation of my nether regions. (As I said to Frank, I didn't know which provided the more striking colour effect: the blue-black of the burnt-out grass, or the area of my upper legs. For several days I would have been more comfortable eating off the mantel.) But the situation with regard to the house was this: that unless we could get the tree debris cleared away jolly quickly, we wouldn't have any workmen left at all. After the fire fiasco, the heating engineer had, in spite of our protests, removed all his men to another job; the electrician was grumbling and threatening to absent himself and his mate until the others caught up with him; and Les the foreman was using the tree man as a peg on which to hang his own woes, and had allowed his boss to remove two key men, the plumber and the carpenter, to another job.

When we protested to Les about this, he stated with dignity that he himself was skilled both in plumbing and carpentry and could perceed with any such jobs unaided. To prove his point, he actually condescended, entirely on his own, to carry out two important tasks that we had been vainly chivying him to get on with when he had a full team. First, he finished tidying, shoring up, and adding what he called the archatriv to the ragged hole which was to be the new door from the new dining-room to the new kitchen. And, even more unexpectedly, he finished connecting the polythene water-pipes from the house-wall and under the driveway and garden wall to the water mains out in the roadway. But, to my chagrin, he now claimed that there was no point in his connecting up the water-services to either the new kitchen sink or the new bathroom until the engineers had connected the radiators (which had not arrived yet); and the electrician was still saying that he couldn't connect the cooker until the sink was connected up.

As for the tree man, we spent several days trying to catch him at home on the phone, and when we eventually did get hold of him, he said he couldn't come back now for a fortnight. The fortnight passed, and we still hadn't heard from him, and whenever we phoned, at whatever time of day or night, his wife said he wasn't at home. Once or twice we were pretty sure that he answered the phone himself, but *he* said he wasn't at home too. We wrote him a letter, but he didn't answer it. Our solicitor, who said it was a waste of time pursuing it further when we didn't have any agreement in writing, was such a gentleman that he never hinted even by an inflection of voice that we were mugs to have fallen for the old 'gentlemen's agreement' lark.

So we set to trying to find another tree man. We eventually located a fantastic old boy with an Irish brogue that you couldn't cut with a tree-saw, who said he would turn up on Saturday and finish the job; and that he wouldn't dream of anything so low as burning brushwood on the site. Well of course he didn't appear on Saturday. After we had given him up, he appeared on the following Wednesday, stayed long enough to provide himself with enough logs for the entire winter, and was off, never to be seen again, leaving us much as we were before we met him. After that we ourselves spent a whole week-end tidying and stacking up in the stableyard any movable or sawable pieces of tree. A few days later, the wife of our 'farmer-tenant' (as we still laughingly called the owner of thirty acres to whom we let our two-acre field), having seen us at work on this project, nobly offered to bring over her hired man with a chain-saw, if she could have any logs she collected for their own fireplaces. To this I joyfully agreed, and the three of us worked really hard for a full day, sawing and stacking and carting away logs. But when evening came, the garden looked as full of tree-boughs as ever. So we had to leave it for a while.

We did ask mamma's treasure if *she* would like some logs from the pile in the stableyard, but she said no, it would be like a knife going through her any time she used a log from those two fine beech trees. She added that we hadn't ought to of cut them down.

She was still spending part of every morning out at the junk-heap, fossicking around for the last dregs of ' my small coal ' and telling me we shouldn't of done it, and I was becoming thoroughly bored with the entire subject of what I should or shouldn't of done. That week-end Frank and I spent some time digging up old fossilised turnips or parsnips from the kitchen garden and piling them, along with the weeds, onto a new compost heap we were starting. That night I had a terrible dream, which I told Frank about at breakfast. In the dream I found her in the kitchen running the old parsnips through the meat-grinder, and when I asked her what she was doing, she said, " I dug these up from your compost heap. You shouldn't of thrown them away. *We* always make marmalade out of them."

It was now the third week in January, and nothing seemed to be moving in any direction. We were constantly confronted with sordid little daily crises and total blocks to progress and petty little wrangles among the three lots of workmen and, to top it all, I wasn't feeling very well. I had chilblains and a septic finger and a particularly nasty runny cold and a croupy cough and a constant dull conviction that before I could get rid of these workmen I would die and be buried in Hucklebury churchyard, so handy across the road. I thought of asking Frank to scatter my ashes up and down Bond Street, but it was too much effort to phrase it well, and I had a morbid fear that he might laugh.

One evening, when Frank had arrived home fairly cheerfully from work, had been greeted phlegmatically by his disenchanting wife, and then, before he got his coat off, had been cornered by all three lots of workmen, each simply bursting with bad news, he joined me in the kitchen, sat on a kitchen chair, found that the chair-back was broken right across, summoned the three foremen again and asked who had broken it, and they claimed that their men were as innocent as babes. When they had cleared off for the night, Frank listlessly opened the newspaper, listlessly laid it aside, and sat staring at the cracked mud-coloured paint of the old built-in dresser. The single overhead bulb swayed rhythmically on its long frayed flex from the wind that blew in around the door, and the old Aga was boiling again with small heart-rending sobs.

I asked him if he'd like me to take up supper. He said he wasn't very hungry. He asked me if I'd like a drink. I told him not to bother because everything seemed to taste of coal-dust and stale tea these days. After a pause I said it was fairly serious if he had lost his taste for food. Frank said it was even more worrying if I had lost my taste for alcohol. We finally agreed that maybe we had both just lost our taste for house-conversion. So he poured us each out a neat dram, and we drank it down and it tasted good. And then I dished up supper and Frank said it tasted fine and ate quite a lot. Then we washed up the dishes in the old stone sink and made our way cautiously up the dark and broken back stairs and along the frigid hallway to the austere comforts of our bedroom, little knowing that the morrow was to bring release from a couple of our problems.

Mark 20th January in red on your calendar, because on that day three more heating men came back on the job, after an absence of two weeks, and what's more, they brought with them the kitchen radiator and the bathroom towel-airer-cum-radiator, and set straight to work installing them. *And* they brought the news that the nine special-size radiators we needed to fit in the window-recesses of all the main front rooms (which last we heard were not to be delivered until 8th March) would be with us early in February. The men even hinted to Frank that if we made an issue of it, they might press for an even earlier radiator delivery. But after talking to Les the foreman, who said that the tree men were holding up completion of the boiler chimney, Frank decided to let it rest for now.

But, most glorious of all, that same day mamma's treasure marched into my kitchen, gave me notice briskly, and marched out again. I had pictured us growing old together within these four walls with never a cheery word between us. All day I was skipping around the house with renewed vigour, singing ' Marching Through Georgia ' to the words, " I'm free! I'm free! The house is ours. I'm free! " This in spite of having eight *tukangs* banging the place down, and the small extra detail that we didn't yet have a kitchen or bathroom or any other room to call our own, or any heat.

That evening Frank, while sharing my joy over my unexpected release, still thought that we should have someone to help with the housework, and suggested I should phone the Bristol Labour Exchange first thing next morning. Which I did. An hour later, while we were still lingering over a late Saturday breakfast, the front doorbell rang, and a pretty little woman with a fresh complexion and soft curling hair stood there. She said she had heard we wanted someone to help clean. I said in amazement, " Are you from the Labour Exchange, so soon? " She looked puzzled and said no. When we had straightened out the double-talk, she told me that she was Mrs Smith, that she lived in a cottage across the village green from us; that the word had gone around the village yesterday that my char had given me notice; that she herself had never had a job in her life, but that she had spoken to her husband about it last night and he had said to go ahead and try for it if she had a mind to. " So," she finished, crinkling her nice eyes with a smile, " here I am." We told her to have a look around at the terrible state we were in and ask herself whether she could cope with such a situation. She smiled again and said, " Well, I could at least polish the brass doorknobs for a start, couldn't I? They look as if they could do with it." As far as I was concerned, she was in! She came to try us out for a week, and had soon outstayed the Man Who Came to Dinner. Before you could say ' small coal ', our two families were pleasurably intertwined. And I wish I could say that we all lived happily ever after, but, life being what it is, we all lived happily for at least a week, before disaster overtook me again.

That week-end, by a final heave-ho, Frank and I succeeded in rolling all the tree-limbs off his so-called grass avenue, though the state of the turf that we had laid so lovingly in November brought from Frank's lips the nearest thing to a whimper that I had ever heard from him. He said it would all have to be re-seeded in the spring, and much of the lawn too. Today we were planting, at last, the hundred baby yew trees in two long soldierly ranks, an operation that was made more interesting by a full gale going on at the time, which blew the little trees out of the icy ground and sent them tumbling across the field before we had a chance to stomp them in. As I said to Frank, it was the first time I had ever chased a tree across a field.

The following Sunday was my Waterloo, though all I did was continue with the harmless practice of gardening. We were out attacking a corner of the garden that hadn't been penetrated by man or beast for a generation, when a branch of rambler rose snapped back, and before I could dodge or shut my eye, it had dealt me a jagged scratch on the cornea.

So far our knowledge of local doctors had been purely academic. We knew that a National Health doctor set up a clinic in our village once a week in the Methodist chapel, if you were lucky enough to have an accident on that day, but Sunday wasn't it. We had also taken the rudimentary precaution of jotting down the names of any doctors we heard of who practised in any neighbouring villages, but we hadn't registered with any of them, and anyway our immediate problem was to find one who would open his surgery right now, in the middle of church time, and not five hours from now. After trying several fruitlessly, Frank ended by getting a name from the police, a doctor we hadn't heard of before, at some distance from us. It was unfortunate, from his viewpoint as well as ours, that, as well as being a practising doctor, he was a practising socialist who was dead set against *bourgeoisie* like us breaking the National Health rules. Before even examining me, he treated us to a little lecture on the glories of the National Health, if only outsiders like us would refrain from having accidents outside surgery hours. Frank then made the dreadful gaffe of offering to pay for this visit as a private patient, and that did it! We had to listen to another lecture on the evils of private patients. He then turned his attention to my eye, which he seemed to dislike nearly as much as he disliked me. During his examination, he didn't address a single remark to me but spoke of me as "she" over my shoulder to Frank, as if I were a dog of no known breed which Frank had brought in to the vet. When he put some drops in my eye, Frank asked what medicine he was using, and the doctor replied, "The correct medicine for the purpose," and we all left it at that. Then he took his hands over to the sink to cleanse them from me, and told Frank that it was all very trivial, that it wasn't anything to make a fuss over, that She wouldn't feel any pain in an hour or so and would be cured by morning, and that he needn't see Her again. That was O.K. with Her.

Early next morning, after a pretty bad night for us both, with me thrashing about, Frank phoned the Bath Eye Hospital and asked the matron the name of the best eye specialist in Bath whom we could consult privately. She gave him two names. He phoned the first one, perhaps getting him out of bed, and the surgeon said cheerfully that he would see us as soon as we could get in. He started treatment on the spot, told us what he was doing and what he wanted me to do between visits, and asked me to continue it for several weeks until he was sure all danger of infection was past. He said it was a bit tricky because the injury was so near the retina, but he was sure we had caught it in time. He endeared himself to me because his first words were, " It must hurt terribly." He asked me to stay in bed for several days to rest the eye, until the pain had abated. He thought I might feel like getting up and resuming a normal life about Thursday, but that he'd like me to keep the eye-patch on during the day until he told me to remove it.

He was right all along the line, but even if he hadn't been, I would probably have got out of bed on Thurdsay morning anyway in self defence, as four of the builder's *tukangs* chose that morning to start hammering on the other side of the partition wall directly behind the headboard of our big bed. (They were thickening the wall to comply with County fire regulations on the depth of wall required between the front and back wings of our house if they were to be used as separate dwellings.)

So there I was Thursday, up and dressed and flying about the house as before, and incidentally interviewing three lots of total strangers, with this villainous black patch over one eye, and on the hour, in the supposed privacy of the bedroom, removing the patch to exercise the eye, revealing what looked like a carelessly fried Polish egg, which all the same seemed to work all right, though still a bit blurry.

One of the three total strangers I interviewed on Thursday was a new candidate whom Frank had unearthed to cart the rest of the tree branches away. Well, technically he was more than a candidate by the time I met him. He had arrived on the premises with his mates and started work, without the formality of consulting me. And the first I knew of his existence, let alone his presence, was when I happened to run across him and Les the foreman entering our bathroom to look for bandages, and they mentioned to me in passing that an axe had glanced off a segment of tree and ' practically severed ' the foot of one of the tree men. So I gave them an old clean sheet to tear up and mop up with, and a car rug to cover the casualty, and they moved so fast that by the time I had hot-footed it down stairs and caught up with the seven-league-booters, they had bandaged and stowed away the victim, started the lorry, run over a nail in our driveway, and were now jacking up the lorry to change the tyre, with advice and encouragement from our gang who were gathered around three-deep.

However, this story has a happy ending, because darn it if the wounded tree man wasn't back on the job next day with the rest of the team! He had twelve stitches in his foot and was hopping around on a crutch, but he was helping to load the tractor with terrific speed. At one point when I was out there directing traffic with a patch over one eye, and this fellow was skipping around on his crutch, we both burst out laughing, and I said that between us we looked like the Spirit of '76. Not understanding my allusion, but eager to take my point, my friend replied, quick as a flash, " Seventy-six what? Trombones? " This made his mates roar with laughter, which was the main thing. Believe it or not, they entirely cleared our place of every bit of tree debris before nightfall. They even swept the lawn with a broom, if you can imagine such perfectionism. I was beside myself with pleasure over it when Frank got home.

By now Mrs Smith had settled in so quietly and naturally that I couldn't recall a time when she wasn't there. Indeed, from the first day it was evident that her job with us fitted her many talents like a glove tailored to her hand. Before a week had gone, she was extending her manifest abilities inside the house to include the great outdoors.

A parcel of one hundred (we bought everything in hundreds these days) Royal Sovereign strawberry plants had been delivered prematurely in the middle of my eye trouble. My natural inclination, nurtured over the years, to procrastinate whenever possible, told me to heel in the strawberries for proper planting later, when both the weather and I were better. But this wasn't good enough for Mrs Smith. She said she would ask her friend Mrs Smart to help her plant them in properly now. Mrs Smart turned out to be just as attractive and energetic as Mrs Smith, and their hard work was spiced with many a merry quip.

During this period, all of us were working hard, including Les the foreman. With the tree debris finally cleared away by Friday evening, we had all (Frank, the engineer, the electrician and I) converged on Les at pack-up time Saturday noon, and cornered him into admitting that the unfinished flue chimney to the heating/hot water boiler was holding everybody up. At first he tried to ride it out by saying that we had our pirorities wrong, and that the engineers weren't nearly ready for the boiler. But he finally gave in and said in a stage-whisper clearly audible to his own men, that the workman nowadays was so mollyclodded that he refused to work outdoors in the winter; that he himself wasn't afraid of a little bit of cold, and that first thing Monday morning would see him out there finishing the chimney, alone if necessary.

Having jockeyed himself into a position that

was unassailable even by himself, he did, first thing Monday, establish himself, alone, on a step-ladder, beside the beginnings of the chimney, on the most biting cold day of the winter. And it was just his bad luck that before an hour had passed, a severe snowstorm blew up which continued for two days. So, too, did Les! He stayed out there all by himself for the whole two days, his nose and ungloved hands blue with cold, the fluffy snow piling up onto his old felt hat and inside the collar of his mac. At first the other men were inclined to laugh at his predicament, but as he stuck it out hour after hour, a grudging admiration crept into their voices, and when finally, Tuesday evening, he came back in, stomping his feet and blowing on his hands and calling for hot tea, and announced, as perky as ever, that the chimney was finished, a great cheer went up from all the men, in which I was happy to join, with tears in my eyes.

On Saturday the heating engineer had laid off his men, to let the builders catch up with him, he said. So now, Tuesday evening, Frank phoned him to give him the glad tidings that the chimney was finished. This was met by a chilly response. The engineer said apathetically that it would be most dangerous to fill the heating pipes with water this cold weather. He said they might freeze and be damaged, and we would be wiser to wait a month or so for warmer weather before starting the furnace. A few brief well-chosen remarks from Frank on the purpose of central heating, to heat a house in cold weather, caused the engineer to change his mind rather rapidly, and he said that he and his men would be there tomorrow with the missing nine radiators.

At mid-morning on Wednesday, Frank phoned from his office to 'satisfy his mind' that the engineers were back on the job. I told him his mind was due for a disappointment; that the engineers hadn't turned up. I asked him if he'd like me to phone them, and he said no, he would enjoy doing it himself. A few minutes later Frank phoned me back to say that the head engineer had discovered last night that the nine special radiators, for which he had accepted delivery a week ago, were the wrong size and had to be exchanged, with another wait. I asked him who was going to break it to Les that he had played snowman unnecessarily for two days. Frank said, "Why not just let him discover it for himself?"

Gently on the Stream of Time

If you do things by the job, you are perpetually driven: the hours are scourges. If you work by the hour, you sail gently on the stream of Time, which is always bearing you on to the haven of Pay, whether you make any effort or not.

C. D. Warner, *My Summer in a Garden* (1871)

Around that same time, early in February, with everything about the house in a state of suspension, waiting for this, that, and the other thing, I started leading a sort of Jekyll and Hyde existence. To put it more mildly and accurately, I sometimes these days put on respectable clothes, hurried out of the house before they got stained or dusty, and went to join with fellow humans for a purpose that was purely fun. It happened like this.

At the end of January, in the midst of the hubbub over my eye, I suddenly remembered that in my not overcrowded engagement-book I had joyfully noted, for the coming Wednesday, an invitation to lunch from the kind and glamorous neighbour whom I called Mrs Bechers-Brook. In view of her always looking so exquisite (even when on a horse, which was how I most frequently saw her, when she passed our house for her morning canter), and because, in addition to my eye-patch and the rainbow colouration of my legs, which still maintained its full glory from ankles to thighs, I had by now developed a real shiner of a puffy black eye spreading out from the eye-patch, I phoned Mrs Bechers-Brook, briefly described the droll mishaps that had overtaken me in my daredevil life, and asked her to excuse me from the lunch party.

She couldn't have been nicer and more sympathetic, and she blessedly didn't urge me to come. A bit later, when we knew each other better, she told me, as a huge joke, that the lunch party was supposed to have been in my honour. But instead of making an issue of this at the time, as I would have been inclined to do, she just waited tactfully until I appeared around the village again without my Nelson badge, and then invited me to another party, for morning coffee this time, with the same guests present, whom she thought I might like to meet.

Having experienced county morning coffee-parties all over southern England from Salisbury Plain to Suffolk, I knew just what to wear on such an occasion: sturdy flat brogues with soles that flapped slightly when I walked, a felt hat so uncompromisingly mannish that it bent my ears down, and the baggiest tweed suit I could muster. At *this* party though, I guessed wrong. I was the only one present who wasn't wearing highish heels, gossamer sheer nylons, a smart Dioresque light wool frock, outrageous earrings, a perfect hair-do, a delicate whiff of scent, and no hat.

I was also a bit slow in getting onto the beam of the conversation. When, for example, one of the wives said that she and her husband had been up half the night with a cow that was calving, and that after all that it turned out to be a bull-calf, I chipped in with, " A boy! Congratulations! " just as all the rest of this knowledgeable crowd started groaning in sympathy with her in her disappointment. As one of the guests kindly explained it to me on the side, " Bulls don't give as much milk as cows."

Another mystery that had bothered Frank and me ever since we moved in—why our mail was sometimes so slow in arriving—was suddenly made clear at that coffee party. A charmer whose name I hadn't caught brought her cup over and asked me, " Why does your mail look so much more interesting than ours? " I didn't have a clue who she was, so I decided to be American and come right out and ask her what her name was. " Britton," she replied. " No, no," I said,

" I mean *your* name, not mine." She said
" Britton " again, and spelled it. My jaw dropped.
In the whole London phone book there had been
only a few who spelled it like that, and here in
the tiny village of Hucklebury there was already
established a real genuine Britton family, who had
lived there for generations. When the postman
saw ' Britton ' on an envelope, he, quite naturally,
took it along to the *real* Brittons to whom he had
been delivering letters since he was a slip of a lad.
To make it even more fascinating, the real Mr
Britton's sister had been the real Nancy Britton
before her marriage, so that anything addressed
like that (say from a bank) sped to the real
Brittons all the faster. The real Mrs Britton said
she also admired the new rose bushes that had
arrived this week.

All in all the coffee party was a great success.
Most of the women hadn't known each other all
that well, being from different villages round
about, and somebody suggested it might be amusing to take turns meeting at each others' houses
every week or so (I strongly urged them to leave
our house until last) until the circle had been
completed. At that another bright soul said we
could call ourselves the Inner Circle Line. And
we were off! This plan was of course a wonderful
morale booster for me, giving me an entrée into
a different charming house each week for six weeks,
and providing a nucleus of warm and helpful
friends whom it might have taken me ages to know
at all well otherwise.

That week also brought my birthday—an

eventful one as it turned out. On the very day, I heard from the family in Boston. I had some gorgeous loot from Frank: a Regency steel firescreen that I had admired in a Bath shop-window the previous week and he had nipped in and bought and smuggled it home; ditto for some Victorian glasses that would be just right for our house-warming if the house ever got warm, and a bottle of my favourite scent. As I said to Frank, I might look like the dickens these days, but I'd at least smell lovely. It being Saturday, he took me into Bath for lunch in the Pump Room, in the sunny terrace-restaurant overlooking the Roman baths and all those statues. After that we took in a good movie.

We got home about tea-time to our frigid love-nest and heard the phone ringing as we came in the door. It was the heating engineer, whom we had been trying to bludgeon into coming out to turn on the heat for more than a week now. He was very grieved; he said he had come out (unannounced) with his men soon after twelve and hadn't been able to get into the house. (I guess I was supposed to stay home day and night to await his advent.) He said he and two men would be along the next day (Sunday!) bringing the nine missing radiators, and hitch them up, on one condition: was the temperature in our house above freezing? If not, he didn't dare risk putting water in the radiators in case they froze before he got heat up. He asked, did we have a reliable thermometer? Frank said yes. The engineer said would he please go and get it and take a reading in our front hall (the coldest room, he thought). So Frank did, and to my surprise it read 33°F. Frank relayed this to the engineer who said they would be out early Sunday. I told Frank I was amazed at it being that warm in the hall; that I'd have sworn it was below freezing. Frank chortled and said he had been nursing the thermometer in his hands all the way downstairs.

Sunday we didn't leave anything to chance. We got up extra early, brought our two electric heaters up front and aimed them at the hall until we heard the engineer's car approaching. Then we speedily whisked them away. This was a good thing, because the first thing the engineer did was check the thermometer in the front hall. It read 34°F. So the men hitched up the radiators to the connecting pipes in jig time, and were just preparing to leave when Frank stopped them and said we thought they were going to turn on the heat. The engineer said airily oh, he hadn't been able to get hold of the electrician today. "Anyway," he added, "you haven't any oil." Frank said with justifiable pride that we had five hundred gallons. (In a mood of unjustified optimism the previous week, we had asked the oil man to call.) The engineer's face fell and he said that in that case he would try to bring the team out tomorrow to test the system.

So Monday early they all turned up. Frank was just leaving for work and he said he hated to miss the fun. I asked him if he'd like to take my place. For a while everybody was milling around like a colony of ants. There was a lot of shouting from room to room, and they all got in each other's way.

During that period, the head engineer and Les the foreman hunted me out, both looking peeved. The engineer said with some choler that he had measured the height for these nine special radiators from a window-recess in the sitting-room; that he had naturally assumed that all the recessed windows were the same distance from the floor, and no one had told him differently; but that *now* Les informed him that the morning-room radiator protruded three-eighths of an inch above the sill and that the shutters wouldn't shut. He said he had suggested to Les that he cut the surplus off the bottom of the shutters. Less chipped in here and said this would be a long and costly job, extra to the estimate of course. He, Les, wanted the engineers to file three-eighths of an inch off the radiator legs. At this, the engineer threw up his hands and said in that case there was no chance of starting the boiler today. This was the umpteenth problem I had been called on to solve that day, and I was getting tired of being King Solomon. So I threw up my hands too, and said sarcastically, " Why don't you dig a hole in the floor? " To my amazement, both men beamed and nodded, and went off, the best of friends. It was apparently a viable solution. The engineer disconnected the radiator from the pipes, Les cut some holes in the substantial old elm floors, and back it all went in no time. I had hoped for one brief moment of glory out of this for having my first bright idea, however unintentionally, but not a bit of it. The two men were busy congratulating each other. There's life for you.

Then we all assembled and somebody turned on the water, and the engineer's own tame electrician, whom he had brought along and who had been fiddling with wires all this time (this sent our electrician off in a huff), gave a thumbs-up to the engineer, who pressed a button to turn on the juice (I felt somebody should cut a satin ribbon), and the whole system started going like billyo. I had been leaning on a radiator in the hall, and I felt so surprised when heat came out that I jumped as if a snake had bitten me. Then all the engineers went away quickly, and we didn't see them again for days and days.

Of course the minute they were gone, all sorts of terrible things started happening, such as the water temperature fluctuating between seventy and a hundred and ninety degrees, and some of the radiators leaking, and at first they had the airstat set so high on the wall (being tall men) that I had to climb on a chair to read it. And for a while there was a phase when the only way you could interest the boiler in starting up again when it had been resting was to turn the stat quickly down to thirty degrees and then up to whatever tempera-ture you wanted. (I was the one who discovered this little ruse, and it worried all the men because it wasn't scientifically sound and shouldn't have worked.) Luckily I was married to an engineer, so he soon had the system working like a dream. But for an interim period, my phone conversations with him went something like this:

N: Darling, the boiler red danger-light is on again.

F: How is the photo-electric eye?

N: *What* is the photo-electric eye?

The boiler provided one or two disappointments for which I wasn't prepared. The three-colour brochure from which we had chosen it in preference to all others, showed a glamorous damsel in evening clothes casually resting one graceful hand on top of this neat slim compact spotless white-enamel box while chatting to some handsome men who were lolling on nearby sofas. Well, as it happened, we could do this damsel one better because we didn't have to entertain our guests in the boiler-room. However, when the boiler arrived I had again admired its pure svelte white-enamel lines and had pictured myself (not necessarily in evening clothes) in one of those ultra utility-rooms that you see in woman's glossy magazines.

The first disappointment came when they installed the boiler carefully in the exact centre of the room. This was presented to me as a *fait accompli*, and my suggestion that they move it over to a side wall was met with a great lack of enthusiasm. The men said with irrefutable logic that it was meant to go in the middle of a room or it wouldn't have had a white-enamel back. Still, all was not lost: I was soon picturing myself sashaying *around* the boiler doing whatever women do in utility-rooms.

The next stage in my disappointment took place the day they lit the boiler. It turned out afterwards that while I was playing Solomon to Les and the engineer, what the engineer's tame electrician had been doing was to hang the enamel box all around with a weird collection of electronic instruments, all of which, I was assured, were essential to the working of the machine, and all of them, I was willing to grant, perfectly lovely instruments; but it was my theory that they ought to be inside, like anybody else's alimentary canal. What I had to face was that the beautiful enamel box was just for show. When the tame electrician had finished with it, it looked just like the White Knight's horse. What is more, if the glamorous damsel tried resting her lily-white paw on *our* enamel surface, she would remove it pretty fast because ours not only attracted a thin layer of oily dust, it was also good and hot to the touch.

I put all this to Frank, and he said *he* hadn't chosen the boiler entirely because of the pretty girl, though he acknowledged her importance; that what had also entered into his calculations was that this boiler seemed to offer the best thermodynamic specifications for our type of house. I agreed that that was nice too.

One alarming side-effect of having the heat turned on, which I for one hadn't bargained for, was the way the walls in all the heated rooms wept. For a century and a half these thick porous stone-rubble walls had been collecting moisture from the chilly air, and now they were trying to release it all at once. They wept as if their hearts were broken. We had to put great wodges of newspaper around the skirting boards to mop up the pools. This went on for several days, and Les had just started complaining that it was holding up the redecorating, when the tears stopped as mysteriously as they had begun.

The redecoration of the new bathroom was slightly delayed because when they had just finished slapping on the second coat of paint, somebody leaned heavily on the new wash-basin which they had installed the previous week, and it instantly broke loose from the wall. This meant that all work on the bathroom ceased while we waited a week for the plumber to turn up. Then, there having been a certain wear and tear on the paint of the walls (the plumber's thumb-prints plus splashes of some unknown purple substance which the men all disclaimed and looked at *me*), the walls had to be painted again, two coats. Les sought me out to tell me that this would be extra to the estimate.

On the other hand, the reason the kitchen was delayed was that one of the painters broke a power-fitting that the electrician had installed only yesterday, and the electrician was so incensed that he left the house in another huff and sulked elsewhere for several days. While he was gone, the builders broke a wall-light connection that he and I had spent some time getting just right. So we had *that* little surprise for the electrician when he returned.

That week the builders broke their teapot, borrowed our kitchen one, and broke that too. As I said to Frank, maybe if they weren't concentrating so hard on their part-singing they wouldn't break so many things.

Anyway the kitchen was a dream. White walls, cabinets lined with Wedgwood blue, pale blue sink and cabinet-handles to match, cherry red lino (the laying of which was a long unfunny story which I will spare you), Wedgwood blue door. The bathroom was all black and white. Both rooms had a large glass-brick window cut into the two-foot-thick outer wall. These glass-bricks looked very cute, but we had certainly fought for them, having ordered them, paid for them, and brought them home ourselves. I told Frank jestingly that I drew the line at installing them ourselves. But that was no jest. One Saturday we came home from Bath to find that the minute our backs were turned they had, quick as a flash, started on the glass-bricks, and actually had them finished, but with the upstairs bathroom window six inches out of true to the kitchen window directly below it. This looked simply peachy. Frank insisted that they reset one or the other of the two windows to match. He didn't care which. Les responded automatically that this would be extra to the estimate, but Frank replied, very short and abrupt, " No, thank you. This one is on you." And it was. So, the masons having departed by then, poor Les himself had to fill in six inches of the stone wall on one side and cut it away on the other side. He didn't have any proper eighteenth-century stone-dust mortar, so he used cement. The resulting mess was always known as ' Les's window '.

It was a wonderful moment when we moved into

the new kitchen and abandoned the old one to the men. They asked if they could use our coal to keep the Aga in for their numerous tea breaks, and they even had ambitions to warm up food (pork pies and the like) for their ' dinners '. I told them this was all fine with me and that I wished them luck in their enterprise, but that ' warm ', not ' heat ', was the operative verb with that Aga and they mustn't expect miracles; I told them that when I tried cooking anything in it, it usually ended up half-cooked. Meantime we sold the Calor-gas caravan-type stove (before the men could break it), at half price, through an ad. in the paper, and were nearly killed in the rush.

Mrs Smith and I spent one whole morning trundling all our china and cutlery forward on trays and arranging them in the new cupboards. It was our proud boast that we didn't have a single breakage. At the end of the exercise, the only thing missing was a favourite little casserole of mine that I used all the time. We asked the men if they had seen it and they all looked hurt and said they hadn't, but I grumbled to Mrs Smith that I bet they had borrowed it and broken it. This went on for about a week until, one day, Mrs Smith came to me wiping her eyes with laughter, and said the men had found my casserole. It had been in the oven of the Aga all this time. It contained some stew that we had had our last evening in the old kitchen and I had forgotten to take it out when supper was over. The men had seen it every day, but there were three lots of men using the Aga now, and each lot had assumed it belonged to one of the others, and it had got pushed farther and farther back. Mrs Smith, on some errand back there, had found the men all peering into the unlovely blackened mess within the dish and had rescued it for me. Still wiping her eyes, Mrs Smith commented, " Well, your stew was certainly cooked through this time."

Our first Sunday in the new kitchen I nearly got electrocuted. I turned on the hot tap with wet hands and leaped two feet into the air with a blood-curdling yell. Frank asked me mildly what was the matter. I told him crossly that it was only that I had had a severe electric shock. He said, " But that is hardly scientifically possible." I replied coldly that in this house anything was possible and that the usual laws of science didn't apply. The next morning the same thing happened to Frank and he discovered that it was scientifically possible, phoned the electrician straight away, and came back with the news that that blankety-blank man had, for some inscrutable reason, earthed the cooker to the kitchen hot-water pipe. Frank told him to come straight out and earth it to something else. Frank then took the electric kettle apart and found that, in changing the plug to the new circuit, the electrician had wired it up wrongly and that this was causing the short circuit. Frank seemed quite happy about the whole situation once he had discovered how it was scientifically possible, but I told him that having Science on our side this once didn't make me a whit less uneasy about the Forces at work in this house.

I said that it was my private opinion that this house had a will of its own, and a keen if Rabelaisian sense of humour. That it positively enjoyed making fools out of us. That it had been getting on fine without us for a century and a half and it didn't like us pushing it around. Frank smiled at me indulgently and went off to the office.

But the fact that forces, other than human, beyond my control, were at work, or at play, in this house was borne in on me strongly a day or so later. A mouse had had the effrontery to appear in our new kitchen. This in itself was a puzzler as the men looked all over and couldn't find any mouse-hole. I didn't argue the point. I just phoned Mr Grits the Grocer, and asked him to send over a mouse-trap. That night we baited and set the trap and left it near where we had seen the mouse. An hour or so later we heard a click and Frank went down and found a little dead mouse in the trap. Because it was late and he didn't want to deal with it then, he put it outside the boiler-room door on top of the tall oil tank. Next morning both the trap and the mouse had disappeared, never to be seen again. That day I phoned Mr Grits for another trap and he said, " But you had one yesterday." So I told him what had happened. He chuckled and said, " Ah, yes. We have very strong mice in Hucklebury."

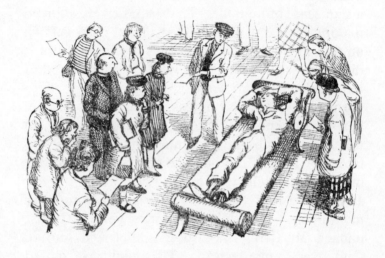

Old Acquaintance

Their joy on this meeting was very great, as well
it might, since they had been contented to know
nothing of each other for the last fifteen years.

Jane Austen, *Northanger Abbey*

Towards the end of February the builders started
a brand-new system. Whereas previously they
had been sprawling their nine men over the whole
house, they now aimed all their forces at once on a
single room. This not only resulted in a very high
concentration of noise and breakages, it also
meant that they were handing rooms back to us
almost quicker than Mrs Smith and I could deal

with them. She and I had calloused knees and broken backs from the constant scrubbing posture. What we had to deal with was, first of all, the honest dirt and general havoc that the men had left us and, secondly, the lack of attention the handsome wide-board hardwood floors had suffered since their heyday in Regency times. The gratifying part was how responsive they were to a bit of loving kindness.

Our routine was this. First Mrs Smith would scrub out the room, then we would both get down and apply a fast-drying floor dye. 'Weathered oak' was the shade we used, though the term described better what the floors were like before we started. Next we both got down again and rubbed in wax floor-polish. It began to be fun when we scooted over the expanses of floor with the dandy new electric floor-polisher Frank had bought us. Then we laid underfelt, and on top of that one of the new carpets which had been delivered that week in tantalising rolls into the front hall. By the second or third room, we had whittled the job down to essential movements and could complete the whole operation in two hours flat (flat on the floor!) allowing time out for a few cigarettes and a lot of groans.

During that period Frank and I were hopping around like fleas. Our first hop, the day after the heat came on, was when we changed bedrooms temporarily from our chilly stronghold at the back of the house to the blessedly warm front spare room, which we declared a prohibited area to builders until they could hand over our real bedroom. We had already taken over the new bathroom and kitchen the minute the barriers were lifted. The dining-room was the next one to be liberated. The builders had lately, since the heat came on, taken to having their tea-breaks here, squatting on the floor and treading in bits of cheese, pork pie, and what not, and Mrs Smith decreed that we must scrub this floor right through *twice* before it was ready for the floor-dye and the polisher. By mid-March the sitting-room was already being painted and papered and was promised to us by next week. And in our main bedroom (which was two rooms knocked together, directly over the sitting-room), the new hand-basin was in and Les the foreman was working on the archatriv of the new entrance door and had started to erect the built-in clothes cupboards that were to extend right across the end of the room. When he let us have that bedroom, we would let him have the spare room, and when he handed over the sitting-room, we would hand over the morning-room. These two direct exchanges promised to be the most hair-raising transactions of the lot, because in both cases Mrs Smith and I would have nine men fidgeting around while we did our soft-shoe routine on the floors and rugs, before they could offload the furniture onto us and get started working on the room we had vacated. Les of course reminded us that any waste of his men's time would be extra to the estimate.

While Mrs Smith and I were in the midst of our floor-polishing carpet-laying project, I had the luck to find the first live beetle (maybe a death-watch beetle?) sunning itself on a window-sill. So I quickly sealed it up in a small tin and sent it to the timber advisers (who were amused that I had put in a morsel of wood for it to munch on). Soon afterward they wrote back that it wasn't a death-watch beetle; that they had found it hard to place, and had had to send it up to London. The letter ended:

> 'I now have pleasure in informing you that we have identified the insect as *Dermestidae*, probably *Dermestis ater*. It is not a wood destroyer and feeds only on woollens, carpets and underfelts, etc.'

Well, *they* may have had pleasure in so informing us, but with some of our new carpets not even on the floor yet, we didn't really share their pleasure.

In case you wonder why I haven't mentioned Frank much in the last few paragraphs, it is because his firm were as good as their word and were sending him off, unpredictably and often, on little junkets, not yet to China or Peru, but fairly far afield in the United Kingdom. On one such jaunt, around the middle of March, his route home passed near to Burford, where we had a friend in the antique business from whom we had bought a few things in the past. So Frank did a detour, stopped in at the shop, and was enamoured of a nice stripped pinewood Regency corner cabinet which he thought would be an answer to my prayer for our dining-room. So he came home and told me about it, and that same night we phoned Burford and bought the piece. When we asked about delivery, our friend said he thought he would be coming our way soon for a sale at Box (five miles from Bath) and would be able to drop it off then, and that he would let us know what day.

The next thing that happened was that Frank found in the local paper an advertisement for a sale of the entire contents of Hazlebury Manor, with viewing on the previous Saturday. So we went over to see it. It was an immense place with I think thirty-two bedrooms and heaven knows how many living-rooms, and before long I had lost Frank on those long legs of his and was alone. Finally I entered an enormous upstairs room with big windows all around, like the Crystal Palace, labelled ' day nursery '. It had a lot of viewers milling about, all looking at a human figure laid out flat on a black and gold Regency catafalque thing— really a fancy sofa—in the direct centre of the room. It was Frank. When he spied me, he sprang nimbly to his feet and strode over. I said, worried, " What was the matter? Weren't you feeling well? " He said airily oh no, he was fine; he was just trying it for size. He said it was listed as a Récamier, that it could hopefully be by Thomas Hope, *circa* 1805, and that if I approved, he'd like to have it for his study. I said that would be fine, if he planned to do his studying lying down. He said he did. So we phoned our Burford friend that same night and he agreed to bid for us. I also asked him to bid for a little Sheraton wardrobe I had seen tucked up in the servants' rooms in the attics. The wardrobe fetched four times the limit I had placed on it; Frank got his Récamier for half of his limit.

The pinewood cabinet was delivered the day before the sale, the Récamier the Sunday after the sale, and in between came the few odd pieces that Bath antique dealers had been keeping for us. When the van driver brought in and unveiled the dining-room D-end table and the six sabre-legged chairs, the moment was almost holy, until Les the foreman, who had been leaning on the architrave of a door watching the performance, said to me, " Glad to see you are buying second-hand furniture. You can save a lot of money that way."

The Récamier, when it came, was even more fun than we had recalled. There were so many niceties about it that had escaped me at the preview: the outward scroll of the headboard, flanked by a pair of gilded eagles' heads; the inward scroll of the footboard, like a Russian sleigh; the gilded lotus-flower legs. At the first chance, we were moved to do a bit of research on it and on Mme Récamier. After looking at the luscious dewy portrait of her by Gérard in the Carnavalet in Paris, we were swayed toward thinking that our piece was French, the legs of her chair were so similar to our sofa. But when we examined the frail, almost spindly sofa in her portrait by David in the Louvre, we veered back into thinking that ours was English. It was an absorbing game.

The moment had come, with the front wing nearing completion, when the wear and tear on our front driveway, from the various quaint equipages that the workmen arrived in, might be saved or diverted if we opened the new back driveway we had planned, which was to start at the old orchard back of the stable, skirt the two-acre field, and, after breaching a stone wall, emerge into the little side-lane running at right-angles to the village green. Weeks, even months ago, we had filled in, in triplicate, the necessary papers, and now came the County's reply. We were stunned: they refused us permission, on the unlikely grounds that we had proposed breaching a wall leading into a main highway. Our little side-lane a main highway? Never!

So I spent the next morning sitting, sewing curtains, in the window embrasure of one of our big empty back bedrooms overlooking the side-lane and, like Bluebeard's sister-in-law, scanned the horizon for anyone coming. At the end of two hours I was able to report that the total traffic congestion over the whole period amounted to two motor vehicles and a horse. The horse was taking Mrs Bechers-Brook on her morning canter, and the two vehicles were the milkman and the baker on their rounds. When I phoned the County Offices to pass on my findings, the official I spoke to had the grace to burst out laughing. He said he would personally acquaint his committee with the results of my survey, and he thought he could confidently promise that County permission would be granted speedily.

Our other adventure, which involved Mrs Bechers-Brook's horse, also happened about then. The two of them cantered as usual past our house, where I was again sitting at the window stitching curtains, and half an hour later, the horse, then riderless, passed again on its way home. Alarmed, I went straight to the phone and tried to ring her house, but when the line was persistently busy, it occurred to me to ring the butcher, whose shop I could see from the window. The butcher's wife answered. She too had seen the riderless horse heading for home, and had tried to ring the house. When she couldn't get through, she had sent her boy down to see if they needed help, but he reported that there was so much commotion down there that he couldn't get much sense out of anyone. He had however seen them organising a search-party of several cars to comb the countryside, and there was some talk of improvising a stretcher.

Later on in the day I ran across Mrs Bechers-Brook in the village. She was looking as blooming and immaculate as ever. When I asked her about the stretcher party, she hooted with scorn, and then, sobering up, said it was terribly kind of everybody; that all that had really happened had been that she had dismounted in a wood to watch for birds, and the foolish horse had taken fright or was bored, and bolted. "Wouldn't you think," she finished, "that some one would have noticed that the reins were through the snaffle-ring?" I said I would indeed, and then sneaked home and asked Frank what a snaffle-ring was.

March was memorable too because we acquired our first gardener, if you could call him that. His name was Tom, he had never done any gardening before, and he showed no overwhelming urge to do any now. The Bristol Labour Exchange sent him along, after apparently finding him unemployable for a couple of months. At his last job, back in January, his boss managed to keep him interested for several weeks before letting him go. (It was Tom's proud boast that he had left that job without getting the sack, and I had a morbid feeling that he was hoping to repeat this triumph with us.) He was a roadmender who was on the verge of achieving the status and perquisites of an old-age pensioner. He could be quite an entertaining talker, if he wanted to and if I could spare him the time, which wasn't often these days, and anyway it wasn't what we were paying him for. His more normal manner verged on the rude. But give him a straight digging job and he was fine, as long as we didn't mind his throwing the flowers on the bonfire along with the weeds. His idea of a really neat bed was one with nothing in it. He came only for a couple of hours now and then (he was afraid of imperilling his unemployment pay), and when Mrs Smith and I were sure he wasn't coming, we would tiptoe out and do the real gardening.

Our project of the moment was to build a rock garden for some of Tia's rare alpines, in the middle of the lawn, to camouflage the two big beech-tree stumps, which I didn't much admire as a natural feature. This involved our humping a lot of largish boulders of Cotswold stone up from the disused pigsties in the broken-down wheelbarrow which Frank by now had put a bottom in, arranging the rocks artistically around the tree-stumps with the grain going the right way, filling in between from a ton of peaty soil we had bought, and, as a start, planting in here and there the fifty alpines we had brought down from the London mews garden. The result was quite nifty, but the job left me so sleepy that, with Frank away on one of his little trips, I was in bed by nine p.m. and went straight off to sleep. When the phone rang, I roused myself to answer it, thinking fuzzily that it was three a.m. and that something terrible had happened to somebody, but it was really ten p.m. and just somebody inviting us to a party.

Thank goodness Frank came home the next day or he would have missed seeing the alpine garden in its pristine glory. The day after that, a herd of cows, ambling by on their way to market, took our open front gates as an invitation to enter. What with their cowman yelling at them and shaking a stick, and Mrs Smith and me rushing out and flapping dusters at them, the cows lost their heads, one of them tried to climb the front steps and enter the hall, some went thundering off over the lawn toward the vine-house, and the most ambitious one of the lot took a running leap to the top of the new alpine garden and stood milling around, dislodging rocks at every step and bellowing her head off with rage and fear. As I said to Mrs Smith, *we* should have been the ones bellowing with rage.

After that we tried to remember to keep the front gates closed.

One day when I was out at the dead bonfire rescuing some plants that Tom had weeded out, I

plunged my fork into the pile, and to my horror a
live snake poked its head out and kept coming
and coming and coming. I left the scene with
remarkable speed, but I told Frank that it was at
least three feet long. Frank smiled tolerantly and
asked me whether I was confusing Hucklebury with
Singapore. But the following Saturday he called
me over to the bonfire pile to see something, and
three guesses what it was. It was the snake-skin
that my creature had sloughed off. Frank took
it into the house and for a long time it was on his
study mantel, and believe it or not it was exactly
three feet long. I didn't go poking into the
bonfire heap much after that, and we never saw
the *ula* again. Frank seemed to take this episode
very calmly, but from something that happened I
surmised that he may have been bragging about it
around the office. The week-end after that, a
friend of Frank's in the firm dropped in at the
house to ask us to entertain a visiting V.I.P. who
was turning up that day. Frank demurred, saying
he had never met the chap, had little in common
with him, and wouldn't know what to talk to him
about. " Oh," the friend said drily, " you could
always tell him about your snake."

On a Thursday evening in the middle of March,
our solicitor phoned from his office to say that the
bank had just returned to him, at last, the stack
of deeds proving our ownership of Hucklebury
House. This was good news indeed. We and the
house were now legally married! The solicitor said
he would prefer not to store these documents in his

office over the week-end, and that to make doubly sure of their safety, he proposed to bring them out in his car next morning at ten o'clock, if that was convenient. It was I who answered the phone, and of course I agreed readily to this plan, but I asked him if it would not save him trouble to send the papers by registered post. The Richard Goolden voice chided me gently for such a rash suggestion, and I quickly gave in, though I told Frank that it worried me to have an old man like that bucking the Bristol morning traffic on a longish drive. Frank said that the old boy would doubtless have been rather hurt if I had put it to him, and that it was best to let him do it his own way. Strangely enough, we had neither of us met our solicitor yet, though we had both spoken to him countless times on the phone, and he had helped us out of many a small scrape over the past months. Frank said he regretted particularly not being here to meet this paragon, but that he, Frank, was expecting visitors to his office who would tie him up all the morning.

At the appointed time, a smart white sports car drew into our driveway, and a dashing black-haired undergraduate-type young man bounded up to our front door. At first I had grave fears that old Goolden had had a seizure during the night. But no. This *was* the real Goolden. It was just that he had been blessed with an elderly voice. Always after that, when I heard the Goolden golden voice on the phone prattling so knowledge-ably of escrows and torts, it wasn't the lithe young undergraduate I pictured, it was still the frail old

Dickensian character with the stiff wing collar and the silver-headed cane, sipping vintage brandy by flickering firelight among his first editions of Trollope and his bound volumes of *Punch*. As Frank had once said, that voice was worth a fortune. This we were to rediscover again and again in the perilous months ahead.

The deeds were divided into two groups, each tied with pink tape. The first bunch were the actual legal deeds, going back to the 1870s, which proved our ownership of the property. I promised Mr Goolden on a stack of Bibles that we would take these in to our Bath bank first thing tomorrow for safekeeping. The other bunch, listed on the receipt I signed as ' and a bundle of old papers ', could safely, Mr Goolden opined, be kept here at home for our own amusement. " Or you could make lampshades of them," the Goolden voice quipped. This bunch were the ones that were fun. There were outmoded deeds going back to around 1793. Before that, there were rent receipts, of five shillings for a half-year, paid to the Earl Radnor, who may have lived in the big house now owned by the Bechers-Brooks. Also in this bundle were the carpentry bills for the ' new ' front wing, dated 1810, covering the previous two years' work, and totalling twenty-eight pounds. This bill covered the fine staircase, shutters, doors and door-frames, floors, everything. ' For a oack dore, 13/9.' ' For puting up stairs & nails, 11/-.' ' For a day self & man cuting posts and puting up privy & nails, 11/6.'

I showed the bill to Les the foreman. He called

all his men from their work, had them gather round, and spoke to them: " Now see here, boys. This here is the carpentry bill for building this fine house back in time immorial. Take a look at what the men were paid, and kindly think of it next time you don't like what I ask you to do, such as working outdoors in cold weather."

A few days later, Les handed over to Mrs Smith and me the last of the front-wing floors (the study floor) for us to deal with. He said he and his men were perceeding to the back wing to orientit themselves with that half of the conversion. This was heady news indeed. I quickly got on the phone to the Aga people to give them the go-ahead for coming out to dismantle and cart away the old kitchen stove from what was to be the living-room of a separate cottage at the back. They appeared the next morning and set straight to work. The most fascinating part (to me) of this operation was that the stove was insulated between its layers with a vast quantity of fine rosy coral, which the men took out to dump by the bucketful on our kitchen garden, telling me (truthfully for all I know) that coral was a wonderful fertiliser. It didn't seem to do the garden any harm and for a while it made it a very interesting and lurid colour.

When the Aga was removed, there remained, of course, the round stove-pipe hole into the big chimney behind. That evening Frank was very curious to know what went on back there. He got a torch and aimed it into the darkness, but he couldn't see much. It was his theory that, with luck, there might be, walled up here, a seventeenth-century fireplace which would be an asset to the room. When he left for work next morning, he asked me to ask Les to break away some of the plaster to see if this was so. Les pooh-poohed this idea to me. He said that as likely as not there would be nothing there, and we would be asking him to plaster it up again, which would of course be extra to the estimate. I kept telling him we would risk this, but he kept making excuses. After this had gone on for several days, Frank came home one evening, saw Les's bag of tools left carelessly open on the kitchen floor, seized a large hammer, and wham! gave the wall a terrific smash. As the plaster fell away, I really couldn't bear to look, wondering what I would say to Les if Frank was wrong. But Frank was right. There stood revealed a fine though simple stone arch about six feet across and tall enough to walk under. It and the huge chimney behind it were absolutely intact. The next morning I didn't say a word about this to Les. He didn't mention it to me either.

Towards the end of March we had the pelmets and curtains up in the sitting-room. Frank had made the wooden pelmets himself by combining and mitring picture-frame mouldings, to the pattern of some pelmets in a period room at the V & A. The curtains were acid-yellow Irish cotton damask, and they cheered the room up quite a lot. We weren't the only ones that liked this room. So did the jackdaws, which had apparently been nested up in this particular chimney since the year dot. Sometimes they dropped down pieces of bread, once a whole loaf, and once they carelessly dropped a live baby (jackdaw), which Mrs Smith and I had a fine time chasing around the room and bagging with an old net curtain. We tried the expedient of having a fire in that fireplace. It made a splendid fire and the chimney drew beautifully, but the only result, jackdaw-wise, was that now they dropped sooty bread instead of clean bread onto the sitting-room carpet.

Then Mrs Smith's friend Mrs Smart had an idea. She said to let her know if an adult bird came down. She had heard, she said, that if you take a jackdaw, put it in a dark room, wait until nightfall, then turn it around three times and let it loose, it will fly off in the opposite direction and the other jackdaws would follow it and none of them ever be seen again.

So when an adult bird came down, we tried it. We caught it in the net curtain, Mrs Smart kindly lent us her coal shed, and we all congregated there at nightfall. We turned the jackdaw around three times in the net curtain (this was the tricky bit; we got a bit dizzy ourselves in the process), and let the bird loose facing away from our house. It turned and flew right back to our living-room chimney.

So Frank made and fitted a tray, painted pale grey to match the woodwork of the room, to slide in inconspicuously just below the mantel and blank off the chimney when we weren't having a fire. That worked like a dream.

In spite of all these goings-on, it was a curious thing that that week, for the first time, the idea of having guests in the house in the foreseeable and even the near future began to sound to me like a feasible, even maybe an agreeable proposition instead of just downright dismaying. It was doubtless as well that I was beginning to feel like this because all our friends in distant parts, and even Frank, were taking it for granted that I would. Frank's immediate reaction, on being told that the sitting-room paintwork was at last beginning to dry, was to exclaim, " Good. We can soon start having people in," a reaction which I didn't share wholeheartedly, because I *had* been having shoals of people (namely, workmen) in, every day for months and months, and *my* idea of heaven was to be really lonesome for a while.

But I think even Frank was surprised at what a wide cross-section of the world wished to stake a claim on our hospitality. When we left London, we had assumed that we would be spared, or deprived of, depending on how you look at it, the great summer invasion of tourists from my native land. Not a bit of it. These same tourists went to London, yes. But now they wanted an excuse to come to Hucklebury, to prove to themselves that such a place existed. American friends wrote that they had heard of our move from friends of friends, and that friends of *their* friends were coming to England and would love to see a place called Hucklebury. From the other side of the globe, long-forgotten kinsfolk in Australia and New Zealand wrote of their burning desire (hitherto well-banked) to visit the homeland. A dearly loved relative of Frank's wrote that ours would be a splendid place for her four children to spend the school hols. A grass-widow in California, whom we hadn't had a peep out of for ten years, said she could spend the entire summer with us if we said the word. (We didn't.) Continental parents hinted that it was their dearest wish for their offsprings to brush up on their English. As not one of these said what there was in it for *us* in any of this, we decided to lie doggo unless they actually appeared on our doorstep.

Even when I grudgingly admitted that I was prepared to remove the barriers for a few choice spirits, we were taken aback at how soon the standing-room-only sign went up for our one (double) guest-room. Like a high-class boarding house, we were booked for weeks ahead.

Tormarton Storms

Any improvement will be temporary.

West Country weather forecast

We were particularly lucky because our first
house guest (if family count as guests) was to be a
young niece, known as Small Fry, who was spending her short Easter school holiday with us,
Wednesday through Monday. Easter came early
that year and fell, appropriately enough, considering the number of things that could go wrong with
the house meantime, on April the first. We were
looking forward to her arrival not only because of
her charms, which were considerable, but also

because she had promised to come clean and tell us all the things that were wrong, from the guest's viewpoint, with our spare room. She produced quite a healthy little list: things like the lights being badly placed and there being no coat-hangers on the back of the door. She had found, without straining herself, about six such items to give to us at breakfast her first morning there, which was an astute move, as Frank set straight to work correcting them.

One item had to wait. We had to report the finale to her by letter after she left. She thought it might protect the top of the little Georgian guest-room chest of drawers from the ravages of uncouth guests (present company excepted) if we had a sheet of plate-glass cut to fit. We highly approved this idea and forthwith phoned the Bristol glass company who had supplied us with glass-bricks (which transaction, it appeared, now entitled us to a charge account). They said they didn't have any new plate-glass of a suitable size in stock at the moment, but that if we didn't object to second-hand glass, they had a good unscratched piece that they could cut to our size and deliver next Thursday. This was when our next guests were due, and it was touch-and-go which would arrive first, the glass or the guests. The glass beat the guests by about ten minutes, and I rejoiced in putting it in position exactly as it was, with ' Britton, second-hand, 11/6 ' printed in handsome big letters right across it in practically indelible royal blue wax crayon.

As Easter week-end wore on, one or two other

suggestions for improving the peace of mind of guests in our house forced themselves on Small Fry's attention. The first had to do with the large urn on a pedestal in the front hall, at that moment filled with forced apple blossom. She suggested that next time I should restrain myself from putting a whole apple tree in the vase as it disconcerted the innocent passer-by, especially at night, to be clutched from behind by a branch.

She also felt that guests would be apt to flinch if I persisted in my present habit of rising to a standing position in the middle of the guest's best story and creeping over to the window-sill. She thought it would be even less reassuring if I explained that I was looking for death-watch beetles. The first time I did this, and popped the creature into a little bottle, it provided some merriment for Frank and Small Fry that my death-watch beetle turned out to be a ladybird. But they laughed out of the other side of their mouths when I actually did come up with not just one but two identical sturdy little brown beetles with cabriole legs (on the window-sill of my up-stairs study) which seemed to us all to resemble the death-watch beetles in the photographs to an alarming degree. So we put them together for company and sent them along to the timber adviser.

Right after Easter we had a letter back. It was not very cheering. It started out, ' Unfortunately both the insects received are full-grown specimens of the death-watch beetle,' continued for two pages informatively and helpfully, and ended: ' As it would appear that you still have an active attack going on in your house, I am afraid that you will have to consider undertaking remedial measures as outlined in my previous correspondence and the leaflets which I left with you. . . .' Frank said, " Cripes," which seemed to cover the situation. He phoned our solicitor, who took a very serious view of the position and advised instituting proceedings against the surveyor. Frank told him to go ahead.

Thanks to Frank's and Small Fry's good teamwork in making the spare room habitable, I could face future guests with a clearer conscience as to their comfort, though there were still frequent barrages of loud hammering coming from the back wing, interspersed with even more distracting periods of complete silence. The trouble was that now that we were no longer living right on top of the workmen, it became rather an over-obvious manœuvre for me to trek back there and check up on their movements.

One day when the silence had continued beyond the point of endurance and I was wondering what nameless catastrophe had overtaken them all, I threaded my way back, past numerous obstacles, found the inside of the back wing empty and echoing, and eventually flushed out three live human beings: Les, his octogenarian tea-maker and our old gardener, Tom, all shacked up comfortably in the stable doorway, sunbathing and playing cards. When I was seen to approach, this idyllic tableau slowly dissolved. They didn't actually rise, any of them, but by the time I was within hailing distance, the cards had totally disappeared and each man had found a sedentary occupation which absorbed him so completely that they collectively gave quite a start when I spoke to them. Tom was honing a scythe (though I had never seen him wield one), Les was assiduously removing bent nails from their card table, an old orange crate, and the octogenarian was, in desperation, polishing the old tin tea-kettle on his shirttail. With regret I refrained from asking Les if the card-playing was extra to the estimate, and confined myself to asking him cheerily where the rest of his team had got to. He confined his reply to saying that they were off on a rush job. When I asked him what had happened to the men who were making the back driveway and the men who were tiling the floor of the old kitchen, Les said he wasn't responsible for sub-contractors and that they hadn't been seen for some days. Then I went away again and, unlike Lot's wife, I didn't look back.

As for old Tom, it transpired later that morning that we would have been better off if he had continued playing cards as, entirely off his own bat, he had had the urge to use the scythe, and had felled to the ground, in a little woodland patch we were cultivating, a number of daffodils in full bud which we had planted in November, some wood anemones, a newly-planted Japanese maple, and three shrub roses which were coming along nicely.

But mostly I didn't have time to worry about what was or wasn't happening to the back wing or the garden. Too many good things were going on in the front wing. The next set of week-end guests had arrived, the ones for whom we had provided the second-hand plate-glass. They were a couple called Skippy and George whom we had been quite thick with in London. At breakfast their first morning, Friday, I was chiding George, an American Air Force colonel, for being unaccountably more interested in visiting Frank's works than in mouching around with Skippy and me. I told him he must be mad, as I could promise him just as much dirt, oil and noise right here at home, far more restfully. Frank interpolated loyally that the works were clean, quiet and free from oil, and that he doubted whether I could produce a Britannia aeroplane for George to look at. Skippy chipped in that she didn't really care about seeing the works (which George said was just as well as she wasn't invited), and that she would be quite satisfied if she saw Frank's office. She said she *liked* seeing people's offices, and she asked me if Frank's was nice. I said I didn't know, I'd never seen it. She looked shocked and said, " Don't you *care*?" I said you bet I cared, but that I knew my place. I said Bristol's was like a very exclusive men's college where you were rusticated if you let a female inside.

The men had it fixed that they would go to the works in Frank's car and leave Skippy and me George's car for the day. At the last minute Skippy, trailing a fetching house-coat, all ribbons and frills, had a bright idea. She said give her five minutes to change, and she and I would follow the men's car in convoy to Frank's office, stay one minute, and then fade away and not bother them any more. Round one to us.

I dashed upstairs to get my coat and handbag. When we came down, five, well six minutes later, Mrs Smith said the men had gone, laughing fit to kill. Round two to them.

It was then that Skippy realised that George hadn't left her the car key. Around this fact we built up a marvellous plan: that we would summon a taxi and have it take us to Frank's office, wait while we collected the key, and bring us home again. Round three to us.

As I hastened to the phone, it rang. It was Frank to say that George was aware that he hadn't left us the car key. I purred, "That's all right, darling, don't give it another thought. I was just ordering a taxi to bring us in to collect it." Frank repeated this to George, and I could hear them both cackling. Frank came back and said that he and George fully appreciated what hardship this would cause us, and fortunately it wasn't necessary: that one of the Company drivers was free, had already left with the car key, and would be with us in ten minutes. Final round to them. As Skippy put it, " You can't win." But I had to tell her that my chagrin at defeat was tempered by the recollection in the midst of Frank's phone call that today was Friday. She asked what Friday had to do with it, and I explained that the village taximan, who also ran the newspaper round and kept a little shop, always shut shop and went fishing on Fridays.

Sure enough, in twenty minutes (not ten, as we were at pains to tell the men that evening) an impressive uniformed chauffeur in a glossy black Humber swept up to our doorway and handed over the key, and the all-male sanctity of Bristol's was once more preserved. As for Skippy and me, we went to Berkeley Castle instead.

This became known as the Key Story, the men claiming that we women told it so many times that week-end to so many different people, improving it at each telling, that it became difficult to recognise the original.

After that came a little gap in the calls on our guest-room. This doesn't mean to say that we were exactly idle. That same Saturday, for instance, stung by an artless remark by Skippy about how pretty the daisies and dandelions looked on our lawn, Frank bought a wonderful gadget resembling a sword-stick that ejected poison into the heart of a dandelion, and when he was brandishing that around, the rest of us did some snappy footwork to keep out of the line of fire.

Also that week-end, on Sunday morning, as soon as George and Skippy left (according to them, it was what *caused* them to leave so early), we prepared and reseeded the grass of the yew alley and the bare patches of lawn left by the tree-fellers. The birds were even more enthusiastic about our project than we were and, summoning all their friends, went to work eating the seeds as we sowed them. To thwart this, we removed the lengths of new netting that Mrs Smith and I had laboriously stretched over the strawberry plants, and laid them over the newly-seeded grass instead. This had the desired effect of forcing the birds to concentrate on the strawberry plants until we could get some more netting.

The big social event of the week, possibly of the century, was that on Tuesday I entertained my chums of the Inner Circle to morning coffee and, as the party progressed, to healthy slugs of dry sherry, as had become the pleasant custom at these gatherings. The two notable features of this affair, other than my enjoyment of it were, first, that we seemed to spend a good deal of our time, drinks and all, in the boiler-room, kitchen, bathroom, and downstairs loo, examining the engineering and plumbing and swapping ideas. As one of the wives said, this was going to prove an expensive morning for the husbands. The second novel feature of the morning was that in the middle of things the Bath antique shop unexpectedly delivered the Georgian sofa-table that we had been urging them to bring for some days now. I was all for having it shoved in a corner to deal with later, but no, the wives all descended on it, helped me unwrap it, and we all started moving furniture around to find the best place for it.

The following Sunday, a friend of Tia's drove her over to us from Devon for lunch. By ' lunch ' I mean that the friend cleverly delivered her to us exactly at the promised time of a quarter to one; that just as the friend had accepted a gin and tonic to keep out the April cold, Tia returned from washing her hands and told the friend quite sharply to set her glass down as we were all going out in the garden. When Frank said that lunch was just ready and suggested that we do the garden after lunch, Tia looked at him as she probably did when he was a little boy and said firmly, " No, it won't do. It looks like rain. We will go out now." So we did. And Tia was quite right. It did rain. About fifteen minutes later the heavens opened. Ignoring this slight inconvenience, she continued her scrutiny of each flower and weed as she squelched along the paths and across the lawn and through the leaky vinehouse and down through the long grass of the old orchard, loving it all and issuing orders like a field marshal, which I, her faithful A.D.C., tried to jot down in a sodden notebook with a damp pencil. Until, as the church clock pointedly struck two, Frank took over and announced with equal firmness that he didn't know what the rest of us were going to do, but that he for one was going into the house, put on dry shoes, and have lunch. I followed him with alacrity, and Tia made a reluctant third. We found the friend, dry as toast, tucked up in the living-room with a book. It stopped raining about half an hour later.

On Tuesday I had a charming letter from Tia. She spoke about how the visit to our garden had invigorated her. She liked the layout we had planned, and she underlined that we must work very hard. I read this in bed, where I had retired with a bad cold. The thought of working very hard didn't invigorate me a bit.

Soon after this, our horizon was further broadened. One of the Inner Circle asked me along to her house in the next village to tea to meet " the Grande Dame of our parish ", as she called her, who took an interest in newcomers and had asked Mary to arrange it. The Grande Dame turned out to be beautiful and witty and hilariously funny, and I came home dazed as if from the sparkle of diamonds. So you can imagine my pleasure when, a day or so later, she phoned and asked if Frank and I could drop in for a casual drink the following evening. The place where we were to drop in turned out to be a stately home standing in sixty acres of parkland, and the casual drink was, of course, champagne served by the perfect butler. Frank fell for our hostess with a thud that was clearly audible, and we had a gorgeous time and came home with an invitation to that great British institution, the formal Sunday luncheon, an occasion too often profaned nowadays, especially in our house, but this time it was the genuine hallmarked article, with the proper ritual of exquisite food offered by soft-footed servants at a long mahogany table to a dozen or more guests capable of good conversation while wearing their best Sunday-go-to-meeting clothes. This time we came home with not only the same sense of exhilaration but with the loan of several books about the history of the district, which had been one of the topics at lunch.

These were great fun, especially *The History of Kingswood Forest* by A. Braine, 1891. It contained a lot of information that was new to me, and what wasn't brand-new gave me the pleasure of recognition of things I was learning already. What he said about our house had amused us all after lunch: ' There is a house of some pretensions near the centre of the village. . . .'

I felt I was on particularly strong ground with Mr Braine's comments on the language of the district, Frank having recently caught me replying to him absent-mindedly, " It do? " And for a long time we had both been ensnared in the meshes of the curious Bristol habit of adding an L on to the end of a word ending in a vowel (mimosal, areal, ideal, etceteral). Quite early on, I asked Mr Grits the Grocer if he had any nice oranges, and he entranced me by replying, " Yes, I have some lovely Jaffals from Cyprus." But the day that British Rail delivered some shrubs and the man commented that they were nice japonicals, and I answered, " Those aren't japonicals, they are camellials," I really felt that I was beginning to belong. I hadn't yet managed to say " I tellee for why " without feeling self-conscious. But give me another few weeks, and I too would be saying fark for fork, laryer for lawyer, a twelvemonth for a year, her instead of she, and I instead of me, along with the best of them, just the way Mr Braine said.

As for the old sayings he quoted, I had delighted in some of them already: Of a man who is stern and sour, they say: " He was brought up on Tewksbury mustard." If anything is lost: " You will find it on Mary Bowden's shelf " (*i.e.* the floor). Another one: " As sure as God's in

Gloucester." One more: "It's as long coming as Cotswold barley." But my favourite was one I had already worked through with Mrs Smith: "a Tormarton rain" (*i.e.* a hard drenching rain from the east). I would ask Mrs Smith after breakfast what the weather was going to be like today, and she would go to a front window and look out at the golden cockerel weather-vane on top of the church. If it faced east she would shake her head and say, " Oh, we are in for a real Tormarton," and I wouldn't start gardening that morning. I asked her what it was called when the cockerel faced west, away from the village of Tormarton, and the rain *still* came down. She laughed and said, " Oh, then it's just an ordinary rain. It won't come to much."

Another part of the church-tower that was sacrosanct was the church clock. It ruled the whole village. The village shops shut for lunch from one till two, and they figured it, not by Greenwich Mean Time, the product of another village called London, but by what the village church clock happened to say on that particular day. If I wanted something from one of the shops pretty desperately at, say, a quarter to one, and while hastening there I happened to meet that shopkeeper ambling home to lunch, it was no use getting excited and showing him what my watch said, checked that noon with the radio pips; he would just smile gently and say that it had gone one o'clock by the church clock several minutes ago. It was a matter of principle, you see. But when no principle was involved, I have known any one of these same shopkeepers to go to all kinds of trouble to open his shop specially and trot out his wares during a week-end or a bank holiday for some guest of ours who had perhaps run out of knitting wool, or who wanted some postcards.

An item in Frank's garden layout, to which Tia referred in her letter, and which we had not yet put into effect, was a great semicircle of shrubbery, across the lawn from and in direct line with the yew alley. When Tia was here, this had been a great semicircle of mud without any shrubbery. On 23rd April (St George's Day; the flag was flying from that busy church-tower), Frank decided to rectify this. He knocked off work early and came out and drove me up to the Forest and Orchard Nursery, fifteen miles away, to help choose some shrubs. We selected about fifteen different varieties (conifers, prunus, dogwood, azaleas, shrub-roses, the lot) and lashed them to the roof of the car, creating a spectacle which stopped traffic in every village we went through. In the gathering darkness, we went right to work planting them, and didn't stop for a bacon-and-eggs supper until ten. Next morning, looking at the result with the eyes of love, we decided that though to the uninitiated it might look like a semicircle of stakes stuck in the ground with labels fluttering, to us it represented sheer beauty.

That week-end we were summoned down to Devon to collect 'a few plants' that Tia had earmarked for us. All day Saturday and up to the moment of our departure on Sunday evening,

163

Tia kept thinking of new plants that we really must have, Frank was digging them up under her supervision, and I was labelling them, wrapping them in newspaper, and staggering off with them to the garden shed. When we got ready to pack up, and really focused on the sheer bulk of the plants crowded into the shed (there were thirty-eight largish shrubs, not counting the smaller stuff), Frank suggested to Tia that we should just tie the shed onto the back of the car as a trailer. As an alternative, I offered to run along behind the car. But all was well. We eventually stashed everything inside, with the larger trees knocking my hat off, resting on my shoulders, or tickling the back of my neck. When we got them home, we rediscovered the incontrovertible fact of life, that it is considerably quicker to pull plants out of the ground than to shove them back in again. But they looked simply marvellous, and the shrubbery actually began to *look* like a shrubbery.

Letter from Tia in response to my B & B letter: ' I am so glad you had that rain while you were digging the plants in. It will do them a world of good.'

Talk about the Crops

At a formal dinner party, talk about the crops
if you must, but never talk about manure.

Advice from Thomas Moore to James Stephens

On May first we celebrated the rites of spring by
having a load of manure delivered. I celebrated
it also by coming down with gastric 'flu. It was
so abrupt. We had a fellow here from Holland, a
stranger to us both, a business visitor of Frank's.
We were all sitting cosily in our sitting-room,
knocking back sherry, preparatory to our taking
him out to dinner. I was speaking very slowly and
distinctly, in an attempt to bridge the language

gap without actually knowing a word of Dutch. (I had asked him if he spoke French, and thank goodness he didn't.) I had put a question to him about delfware, and while he was framing his reply, I rose wordlessly from my chair, left the room, and was seen no more. Frank, poor chap, eventually took the man out to dinner alone, but I was beyond caring.

The next day I was still laid low, and the question then arose as to what we were going to do about a couple from Boston, Lois and Jim, who were due to arrive at our place via Germany on the Thursday, and who were incommunicado meantime. Frank refused to get excited about it, and said soothingly that on the day he would decide whether he would meet them off their train at Bath and give them a meal there before bringing them out to hand me a lily, or whether to send them word at the airport asking them not to come. However, on Thursday morning I suddenly felt grand again, just a little wobbly, and decided to go with Frank to meet their train.

They arrived on time, and we took them to a Bath restaurant, the Hole in the Wall, which has very rich gourmet food, some of it laid out appetisingly on a long table almost within grasp of the clients. I was starved, my first meal in several days, and I was tucking in so enthusiastically that I didn't notice for a while that Lois had gone very pale. Darn it if *she* didn't have to leave the restaurant and lie down in the car while we scraped our plates clean. By the time we got home, she had rallied.

The third thing that happened, in case you are superstitious, was that as we were getting ready for bed, Frank sneezed a freak sneeze that dislocated something and he couldn't straighten up properly for a week. So I had to give up being an invalid. There was too much competition.

In spite of all these hazards, Frank (being brave throughout and not letting anyone *mention* his ailment) drove us to Berkeley Castle, the Slimbridge bird sanctuary, and Wotton-under-Edge (pronounced Underij) on Friday, and to Laycock Abbey by way of Bath on Saturday. On Sunday they had to go. They were very nice appreciative guests and we enjoyed them. After they left, I persuaded Frank to take a course of treatment at the hot springs in Bath, which are a chapter in themselves. Wonderful place. And that did the trick.

Lois and Jim had boasted of being do-it-yourself fiends, and while they were with us they had somehow talked us into believing that it would be a cinch for us to re-cover Frank's Récamier ourselves, using the roll of exotic French black velvet *moiré* we had bought for the purpose. Indeed they had gone so far as to say that they would do it for us if we could collect two items of equipment which they jotted down. This sounded easy, and on the Saturday morning we had sidetracked through Bath to try the two biggest drapers' shops, with a total lack of success.

We found this such a challenge that, even after the guests departed and our zeal for home upholstering had cooled below blood heat, the search continued of its own momentum right into the following week-end. And where do you suppose we found and bought the robust wide black linen tape, for which we had hunted in vain all over Bath? In the little drapery shop in our village, where Lois had found some knitting wool she had been looking for everywhere.

Finding the right kind of gimp tacks (which of course turned out to be called something entirely different in England) also had a story attached to it. About the tenth place we tried in Bath told us of one more faint hope, a small upholsterer's shop on the other side of an old bridge that we didn't even know existed. With the aid of a sketch drawn on a scrap of paper by our informant, and a good deal of to-ing and fro-ing, we tracked down this shop, which was so crammed with junk that the quest seemed hopeless. But in a trice the shopkeeper opened, first shot, the correct little drawer out of a myriad of possible ones, and measured out to us, as if they were gold-dust, a penn'orth of his pre-war stock, now irreplaceable as the factory had been bombed all those years ago.

Having gone to all this trouble to obtain for ourselves the right do-it-yourself equipment, we cravenly asked the old upholsterer whether *he* would re-cover the Récamier for us. But he waved in despair at the furniture crowding his shop and told us that he might not complete the work he had on hand for a twelvemonth. We asked him to phone us when it was our turn, but he said he didn't have a telephone.

So we acknowledged defeat on that score but

victory over finding the gimp tacks, and tried to fight our way back into town. This took us through such a maze of befuddling crooked old streets that we completely lost our bearings, and to our intense surprise we suddenly emerged, under a railway bridge, into the thick of the Saturday morning traffic, going the wrong way on a one-way street with the lights against us. In the centre of the road a traffic policeman stood regarding us more in sorrow than in anger, raised a white glove to stop us, and strolled over. " I suppose you know," he remarked conversationally, " that you are breaking every known traffic regulation. How on earth did you manage to get into this position?" Frank explained. The policeman said, " I believe you, thousands wouldn't," and waved us on.

In the evening Frank, as if to prove how much better his back was, had his first session that spring with the old motor lawn-mower. By a miracle of patient tinkering he wooed the sullen engine into croupy life and rode it like a bucking broncho for an entire circuit of the lawn, to the cheers of Mr and Mrs Smith and me. " We'll make a farmer out of you yet," Mr Smith said, causing Frank untold pleasure.

The next thing that happened in our busy busy life was that one evening that week Tom, the old gardener, talked himself out of his job with us, if you could call his reluctant approach to any form of work a job. He sassed me once too often and made the mistake of doing it in Frank's presence. When Frank asked him gently to mind his tongue, he sassed Frank too, and was out of our employ with breathtaking speed.

During the brief hiatus between gardeners that ensued, the rhythm of our life remained undisturbed (or disturbed, as the case might be). That same evening, for instance, we planted a tree, a beautiful weeping pear that had arrived that day from Forest and Orchard. We placed it in the bed to the left of the top of the yew alley, to balance asymmetrically the old weeping ash to the right of the alley. This old ash was one of the joys of the garden. It had a personality for each season. As it stood now, in late spring, its umbrella of new leaves, sweeping nearly to the ground, already concealed its inner structure of branches, and made a delightful hiding-place for any children who came to see us. But in winter, when its leaves had fallen and its structure was laid bare, the weird serpentine convolutions of its old branches made for a different sort of pleasure. At one point a gnarled bough, as thick as your arm, divided into two and a bit farther on joined into one again, causing a musical friend of ours to call it the Ophicleide Tree.

A shopkeeper in our village, whom we admired for his spunk under adversity, had had a twisted leg since birth. And he told us that when he was a small boy, early in this century, a Colonel Gordon, who then owned our house and was a great gardener and was called " Squire " affectionately by half the village, had lifted the little crippled boy onto his shoulder, taken him into the garden and under the umbrella of the ash tree, showed him its twisted branches, and told him that of all the trees in the garden, this was the one that the birds liked best to nest in.

Mrs Smith found us our next gardener, though she didn't know him. She had heard that this nice man, a retired widower, had recently taken a room at a nearby farm and gave them an occasional hand with the work. So we went along to see him. He said deprecatingly that he wasn't much of a gardener, but that he had lately become rather a dab hand at repairing dry-stone walls. At this we snapped him up. We privately called him Mr Chilprufe because he was out in all weathers. He proved to be a bit of a homespun philosopher. One day I went out and found him standing quite still, in the slight drizzle that was falling, puffing at his pipe and contemplating the tumble of fallen boulders beside the wall. Then, without haste, he leaned over and chose a great crooked brute of a rock, and neatly fitted it exactly into an aperture in the wall. I applauded. He smiled slowly and remarked that rocks were like people: that if you looked hard enough, you could find the right place for them all. When Frank came home that evening, I told him this story. He had had a trying day at the office, and he replied that this might be true of rocks, but that it certainly wasn't true of people.

After Jim and Lois left, we had given up house guests for a while, the way people give up candy for Lent. We just had too much to do to afford the luxury. The only snag was that guests didn't give *us* up. Whereas in London our chief bane, from out-of-town and overseas visitors, had been guess-who-this-izzers on the phone without prior warning, in the country the same sort of visitor considered it the O.K. thing to do to come knocking at our front door, crying " Surprise, surprise "; or if no one answered the door, it was considered a fair do to go roaming around our garden in their best clothes until they dredged me up, in dirty old jeans, hiding in a weed-patch, and to explain this breach of my privacy by saying that their mother, or aunt, or great friend Mrs Whoozit, back in Toonerville, had insisted that they look us up. Then I, that lovable old duffer, would have to ask them inside and, one thing leading to another, it would usually end with our offering them food. This could run us into quite a tidy little bill, over the weeks, at the Hole in the Wall, and an even bigger, less scheduled hole in our time, especially if I prepared a meal for them at home.

The sort of visitors who would allow themselves to get into a situation like that would probably also be such that, in spite of any protestations on my part, the wife would come right into my kitchen, which any fool could see was tailored for one cook only, and stand squarely between the cooker and the sink while I was trying to take up the rice, either giving me her lowdown on That Man in the White House or, worse still, lowering my morale by telling me of her far superior way of cooking rice. If, at this point, Frank should gallantly lead the lady away for a drink, either she would be impelled to carry the drink right back to the kitchen to consume there, or if by some fancy footwork I could forestall this by bringing my drink into the living-room, I would catch her eyeing me up and down furtively before remarking thoughtfully on how English I had become, an observation which never failed to send any British subject present into convulsions of mirth, and which I could tell right away was not intended by the guest as a compliment to me.

Most of our local best friends were blessedly too frantically busy to indulge in dropping in on neighbours, unless they were selling tickets for their favourite charity, in which case all they wanted was the cash and then good-bye. But there was one terribly nice Service wife living some distance away in a big house well provided with batmen, and her particular lay was to leave me be all day, and along about five p.m., when all godfearing wives without benefit of a batman-cook were beginning to think what to give their husbands for dinner, unless they were beginning to think what the hell they were going to wear to some party that evening—along about that time, this footloose wife would turn up with monotonous regularity, hoping for a cup of tea or a drink while she related her latest problems with the batmen.

On one such occasion, I had had an unexpected invasion of friends of friends from America neatly timed for lunch, and after clearing that all up, I had just got around to doing the day's washing and was out in the boiler-room hanging up clothes, with the back door ajar to relieve the heat. When the front doorbell rang, I froze like a statue, clasping the bowl of wet clothes to my bosom. The bell pealed out again and again, and still I stood. Then, to my horror, I heard little mincing steps approaching, and a jewelled hand thrust the door wide open. Mrs Batman and I were eyeball to eyeball with each other. " Why, hello," I heard myself saying heartily, " I thought the doorbell was someone else." She didn't stay for tea or a drink that day, and she didn't drop in again. But we made a point of asking her and her husband to a formal dinner party soon after that, and she made a point of returning our invitation in kind with admirable promptness.

When I say ' formal ' dinner party, I should have explained earlier that unless something special was afoot that I knew about in advance, Mrs Smith came to me for only two or three morning hours, three times a week, pummelling two or three rooms into glistening shape each time. But around then I was beginning to be acutely conscious that we were indebted to an awful lot of nice people for slap-up dinners for which a pot-luck meal would not be an adequate substitute. In our Service life in out-of-the-way places, I had become accustomed to the hot-hostess act of preparing, or helping to prepare, a three-or-four-course dinner, changing quickly into something dressy, greeting the guests and, when we had sat down at the table, trying to act surprised at what we were having to eat. But one great thing, among many other things, about Service life is that, be it ever so humble, or humbling, there is always at least one erk in the background who can be dragooned into taking up the soup, announcing dinner, serving and changing the courses, passing coffee, and washing up afterwards. In carrying this out, the erk may of course introduce unrehearsed variations to the prepared routine, such as spilling new potatoes down the cowl neckline of the C.O.'s wife, or falling flat on his face with a tray loaded with drinks. But it was certainly better than any alternative I could think up.

In wondering whom I could dragoon this time, the mind of course immediately leapt to Mrs Smith and Mrs Smart. But how would they feel about it? I needn't have worried. They both thought it was a smashing idea, so long as they didn't have to do any cooking. So next time I was in Bath I got them each a smart navy nylon uniform at Jolly's with a frilly white apron, and when they got all dressed up, they looked as cute as maids in a Feydeau farce. We started out easy with a big cocktail party, which we all enjoyed enormously. The girls came over in the afternoon and we all made fancy *canapés*. As for the first dinner-party, we were in clover, because in her giddy girlhood Mrs Smart had had a brief fling as under-maid in a great house and knew all the mysteries of waiting-at-table, so she could coach Mrs Smith, who was a quick learner. But nevertheless, at the girls' suggestion, we had an undress rehearsal that afternoon, with the table all laid, and me sitting at my place at the long table helping myself to imaginary food from an empty platter held at the right level by each of the girls in turn.

In the event, we would have two platters for

each course, so that the girls could start serving from both ends of the table at once, before the food got cold. There was one thing Mrs Smart had to unlearn from her great house: in our not-so-great house, we stuck to the American custom of serving the hostess first. This was so that the server could hiss into my ear if anything terrible was happening in the kitchen, and I could gracefully arise and go off and shoot myself.

In practice, only one grade A terrible thing happened that I can recall. Just before announcing dinner one time, Mrs Smith came into the living-room unexpectedly, said smilingly to me in a low voice, " There isn't enough soup to go round," and I skipped out to the kitchen like a shot. But all was well. It was just that there were two double-boilers on top of the cooker, the big one with soup, the small one with spare sauce for the chicken, and they had confused the two. My fault entirely. I had forgotten to tell them. So they just poured back the chicken sauce into the saucepan, rinsed the soup bowls under the tap, and Bob was our uncle. Oh and one other time the girls absent-mindedly started offering the platters before they had passed the plates, but the guest of honour said he thought we were just starting a new fashion of eating off the linen place-mats.

Only one party we gave made the girls unhappy. I thought it might be easier for them if we tried a serve-yourself buffet supper. This meant that the poor girls were cooped up in the small kitchen, waiting to serve coffee, and they hated it. They said they kept hearing bursts of laughter, without knowing what was funny. So I didn't try that again.

Another experiment we tried only once was the picnic supper with the keg of cider. Of course it rained that evening and we had to have it indoors, which was to be expected. But the cider was a disaster. I don't mean that people didn't like it. They maybe liked it too well. After the meal they started curling up in their chairs and yawning. One woman whom we knew very slightly actually took off her rings and wrist-watch and laid them neatly on a table as if it were bedtime. When it came time to go home, which seemed to come pretty late, three people forgot their umbrellas although it was pelting with rain outside, and one man managed to forget his mackintosh. When they all came around next day to collect their things, they said they couldn't imagine what had got into them.

With all this new burst of activity on our part, in a new community where most people knew each other better than they knew us, it was inevitable that I should occasionally get guests mixed up with each other. Being not very bright in this line to begin with, I was sometimes guilty of, say, introducing a man to his sister, when she had a different married name. So it was a great comfort to me, when we were asked to dinner at a neighbouring farmer's that he several times fumbled over my name. About the third time he did this, he turned to me and said, " Why is it, when I can remember the names of all my sixty cows, that I can't remember your name? "

Useful versus Agreeable

To . . . blend the useful with the agreeable has
ever been considered a difficult but an honourable
task.

George Hepplewhite (1788)

The month of May went out with a bang for us
because of two important events, one wholly
agreeable, the other strictly utilitarian and disagreeable. The two didn't exactly blend, but
they did at least counterbalance each other to
keep us on a more even keel, somewhere between
drinking champagne and taking arsenic. To deal
with the disagreeable event first: it was during
that last week in May that we had to make the

178

crucial decision to fumigate the whole house with cyanide for death-watch beetle. It was also during that week (*olé!*) that my book came out.

For some time now, death-watch beetles had ceased to be a subject for levity with us. If we found one on a floor or window-sill, we no longer joined in a raucous Bronx cheer. There were too darned many of them for that. We just added it to the others in the pill bottle and tried to forget about it. When we had totalled thirty from various rooms in the house, Frank phoned the timber adviser, and he came straight out to see us. He clinched our fears by confirming that they were all full-grown death-watch beetles keen on raising large families.

So there was no longer any question of *whether* to fumigate. We would have to do it and like it or lump it. We would, the adviser said, have to take down all curtains, roll up rugs and under-felting, prise up a floor-board in each room, front and back wings alike, and remove to our new garage all mattresses, pillows, bedding and all foods except tinned things and bottled wines. I asked him about clothing, and the adviser, an undoubted enthusiast in his field, said happily no, to leave them hanging in opened cupboards, that the great thing about cyanide was that we would never again be bothered with clothes-moths. Well, as I said to Frank afterwards, it seemed rather a cumbersome way to get my fur coat mothproofed, but that I was always ready to accept any crumbs of comfort along life's path.

As to the routine of fumigation, the adviser said

that the premises must be cleared of people for a week; that the County Medical Officer would seal the gates and affix danger notices; that the men, after sealing all windows, outside doors and fireplaces, would (wearing gas masks and protective clothing) release a high dosage of hydrogen cyanide into all the rooms for seventy-two hours, then unseal and open the doors and windows and let fresh air in for another seventy-two hours. During the whole period, three men, who would pitch a tent in our garden, would take turns being on guard, night and day. At the end of the week the County Medical Officer would return, test the safety of the house, and unseal the gates. I thought of asking how the Medical Officer could get in to examine the house with the gates sealed, but I decided it wasn't my problem.

The question then remained: *when* would we do it? I was all for getting it over with right away. But the adviser was in favour of our waiting until sometime between late June and late July, to ensure that any sleepy-heads in the beetle world had fully emerged from hibernation. Frank contributed that we must fit it in at a time when he was not away on a trip; that he was slated to go abroad several times over the next two or three months (which was the first I had heard of *that*!) and that he would try to tie his Company down to exact dates. I said drily that I too would like to hear the exact dates.

Then somebody had the bright idea of wondering what we were going to do about the workmen in the back wing, who still came in from time to time, so it seemed to us, as the mood struck them, to do a little desultory hammering. What we wanted, of course, was to have them finish the job and pull out. But how could we achieve this? As soon as the adviser left, we went back and Frank tackled Les, telling him bluntly that he and his men must be finished and out by the end of June, and explaining why. Les replied promptly that what Frank asked was quite out of the question; for one thing, they had the redecorating still to do, and he knew for a fact that the painters and paperers would be busy on other jobs for weeks to come. " Good," Frank said briskly, " that is exactly what we wanted to know. That being so, we will delete all painting and papering of the back wing from the estimate." Les was so taken aback that for once he didn't have a ready reply.

When we got back to the front (if you know what I mean), we ran across Mrs Smith and told her our woes. " Oh, don't worry about the painting and papering," she said serenely, " Mrs Smart and my father and I can paint and paper the rooms back there if you want us to. We do her house and ours every year." Now *we* were the speechless ones. There was no end to the skills of Mrs Smith. She was a regular Mary Poppins.

28th May was the official publication date for my book. We had known this for several weeks, but had supposed it to be just an abstraction like the North Pole (no pole) or the International Date Line (no line). Not a bit of it. True, they sent me my free copies of the book on 8th May, asking me not to distribute them among loyal relatives until the 28th. But the publisher made a pleasant little occasion of The Day by sending me not only a charming pep letter, but a spare batch of the first reviews. He had suggested earlier that we might like to hire a press-cuttings agency to send us reviews, but we didn't suppose there would be many, and I wrote him back that we were scared it would make too depressing reading.

We hadn't happened to mention my writing a book to any of our particular friends. But one day a week or so later Mrs Bechers-Brook hailed me in the village and asked me quizzically whether it could be I whose book was reviewed in today's London *Times*. I was so flustered that I forgot to ask her what the *Times* said, we being *Telegraph* readers. And when, that evening, Frank, who was as curious as I was, asked the local newsvendor for one, he was out of stock, and threw up his hands at the idea of getting us one.

The following Saturday (Frank's mother had come to us for the week-end), we were all invited to the *real* Nancy Britton's for tea, in a lovely big Georgian house just outside Bristol. And the first thing that Frank, that bloodhound, saw on entering the house was a stack of London *Times* in a corner of the living-room. At the first opportunity (Frank's mother and the real Nancy Brittons' real mother were carrying on a conversation of their own with me in the middle) Frank took the real Nancy aside and asked her if she had the *Times* for the 14th, and told her why. They went to look on the corner table, and that was the only *Times* for the week that was missing. So they went and sought out Winnie, the family's friend and housekeeper, and she entered the chase. She thought back and decided that that was the day she had taken the *Times* to fold on top of the boys' winter clothes when they came down from Eton. So up they all went to the attic, the boys having meantime joined the hunt. And sure enough, there it was in a trunk, folded as neatly as could be. Nancy was all for dashing down with it to surprise me, but Frank, with that endearing caution of his, said they had better read it first, and if it was very bad they could pretend they hadn't found it. It was short, but nice enough to please anybody.

On the Monday, Frank's mother returned home, and Frank left for America. As for me, I stayed at home with the strawberries. It was a wonderful year for strawberries, which meant that ours were gorgeous, and so were everyone else's. In other words, there was no market for them. At any rate, not in the two swank greengrocers' shops in Bath that we sometimes patronised. When we had taken some sample punnets in with us on the Saturday morning, one of these two shops wasn't interested at any price, and the other shop offered us one shilling and sixpence per large punnet—a derisory price since ours were better than the ones they were selling at four and six a punnet. So we brought the dozen sample punnets back home.

In a moment of optimism, we had bought up a small quantity (half a gross) of empty punnets from a Bristol sundryman, and it looked as though we were stuck with them; until I told our sad tale to Mrs Smith. She of course had a solution. She said if I liked she would take the dozen punnets home with her, and lay them out temptingly on a table just inside a big window she had in her cottage opening directly onto the road near the bus stop, with a sign saying two and sixpence per punnet. They were gone in no time, and on Sunday Mrs Smith came over wanting some more. But what with my mother-in-law visiting us and Frank leaving for America, I told Mrs Smith that we'd lay off for a couple of days to let me catch my breath. On Monday she was at me again, and as soon as I had waved my two voyagers away, we went out and filled another dozen punnets. That did Mrs Smith until Tuesday evening, when she took so many advance orders at her weekly whist drive that she told me she wasn't putting the punnets in her window any more (" not selling them to strangers ", was the way she put it). By now she was wandering in and out of our gates any time of the day or evening to fill what she called " my specials ". As of Wednesday evening she had sold a theoretical fifteen pounds of strawberries, except that, as she pointed out, it wasn't anywhere near that poundage because she was continually reducing the amount in each punnet as orders increased.

By this time she was doing all the picking herself—she and her young daughter and her father and Mr Smith and Mrs Smart. I suggested she should pick all the ripe strawberries there were every two or three days, but she said no, they were fresher this way (also I guess she enjoyed it more this way). By Thursday we were having a punnet crisis, and Mrs Smith was rushing around among her ex-customers wrenching the empties away from them to fill and sell again. I suggested she should put a sign in her window offering a halfpenny for empties (which was about half what they cost new) and she said scornfully, " And have everyone from here to Tormarton bringing in their dirty old ones? No thank you. We only want our own back." In the end I had to phone all over Bristol to get another half gross, most dealers having sold out.

At each picking there were a certain number of small second-rate misshapen berries, but still ripe and of delicious flavour, which we tossed into a separate basket and afterwards decanted into a big glass bowl in the kitchen. The scent, which was intoxicating, spread right through the house to the front door. Of these berries, Mrs Smith took what she wanted for jam and, as the quantity of those she didn't want mounted up in the kitchen, I began casting about desperately for a way *not* to make jam of them. My theory was that if I started making jam over a hot stove in this beautiful weather while Frank was off sampling the fleshpots of America, I would start feeling sorry for myself, which would be bad for us both.

Fanny Farmer in her *Boston Cook Book* provided the perfect solution with a thing called Tutti-Frutti, in which, by a not too complicated procedure involving a fair amount of brandy but no cooking at all, I could, with luck, end up with a single product almost as good as the original strawberries and the original brandy. With this recipe it looked to me as if I might get through the entire summer without washing a single preserving kettle, scalding a single jam pot, or rigging up a single jelly-bag, the only snag being what I was going to say when Frank asked what had happened to his bottle of V.S.O.P. Rémy Martin.

But the fine thing about the recipe was that the initial pint of brandy went on forever like the widow's cruse, and actually increased in volume as the days went by. Another great thing was that if at any time of the day or night I began feeling the tiniest bit low, I could mosey down to the kitchen and give the mixture its daily stir, licking the spoon carefully afterwards, and up would go my spirits! It was also an inspiration to see how those miserable little deformed berries improved in appearance as they got a noggin of best brandy under their belts. Day after day they grew rosier and plumper, and, I might add, more delicious, tasting exactly like Rémy Martin laced with strawberry, instead of the other way around. This would go on for a week or so, when they didn't exactly explode, they just sort of deflated like a tyre with a slow leak, and if you could catch them just before they did that, you could skim them off, without extra juice, into an un-scalded jam-jar until you wanted to use them. If you left them floating around indefinitely in the big stone jar (I used a large baked beans pot), they gradually shrivelled up and became less interesting to eat, though the gravy was divine.

I figured up that next year, when the fruit season rolled around, all we would need to do was to strain off the old fruit and start again with a pint of the home brew, the surplus of which meantime, with any luck, had been adding zest to the punch-bowls and mulled clarets of many a fête-day.

Before Frank left for America, he had consulted his diary and his boss and his crystal ball and, among us (us including the fumigation company by phone and Les in person) we had fixed on 29th July for the start of Operation Cyanide. Mrs Smith had also consulted with her family, and had come back with the suggestion that they leave painting and papering the back wing until after Frank returned from America, and perhaps until after the fumigation men left. Mrs Smith and I were in favour of the latter course, to avoid the risk of dirtying up new paint and wallpaper, and Frank said anything we decided was fine with him.

As for Les's departure, he remained a mystery man to the end. The Saturday before Frank left for America, Les had told him, in answer to Frank's earnest enquiry, that he couldn't say when he would finish the back wing. " It could be a week, it could be a month " were his exact words. Three days later, on the Tuesday, Les found Mrs Smith out at the strawberry patch (I had gone indoors for a minute to answer the phone), handed her the key we had lent him, and silently stole away (or, to be exact, got into his old jalopy and back-fired his way down the drive). We never saw him again. The place didn't seem the same without him.

For quite a while Frank and I had been aware that dear Mr Chilprufe, though a first-rate philosopher, wasn't much of a speed-merchant as a stone-wall repairer. From a friend we had heard of a wonderful family of stone-masons, perhaps third generation, whose wives and mothers made a principle of producing nothing but boys, who all looked exactly alike (tall and rangy and good-looking), and were all top-notch at their job. And before departing Frank had said that if Les and his boys should finish while he (Frank) was away, I should ask the Hembroughs (as they were called) to drop round and survey the stone work we needed doing. So I phoned them, and no less than three Hembroughs turned up, carbon copies of each other. This made for a splendidly comical routine, which they relished to the full. I would say to one of them that he had told me such-and-such, and he would say, " No, that must have been my brother," and the brother would say, " No, I think it was my nephew," and they would all fall to laughing, shaking like aspens, without uttering a sound. Later, when we had about six identical Hembroughs working on the premises, branching out as far as second cousins, this game offered even greater possibilities. I was so taken with the charms of this family that on my own initiative I asked for a few of them to come over one day and try out mending a section of stone wall on an hourly basis, for me to show Frank when he got home, and meantime for them to estimate for moving that old medieval stone archway that

Frank was so dippy about, from where it was, tucked away in a corner, to the bottom of Frank's yew alley, breaching the six-foot high stone wall that led to the old ' tennis court '. I didn't know how I would break it to Mr Chilprufe that we were taking his anthropomorphic boulders away from him, for the moment anyway, but I put it to him on the basis that we needed him for the gardening, which was certainly true, and he took it as philosophically as any old Greek.

During the trial period, the assorted Hembrough boys were such a joy to have around, so quiet and polite and hard-working and somehow predictable, that I gave them a little verbal testimonial to that effect, saying how easy they were to work with. They grinned appreciatively, and one of them, a nice lad in his twenties, said, " You amaze us, Mrs Britton. Most people hate us," and he turned to the lad working beside him (maybe his brother or cousin) and added, " Don't they, John? " John nodded gravely and said, " Yes, most people despise us." And the whole lot of them went off into that shaking silent laughter again.

While Frank was away, people were very nice about asking me over for meals. On the first occasion, I was the only non-baby-owner and non-dog-owner present, and as the table-conversation ranged from how to bring up wind in babies to how to cure hard-pad in dogs, I came home feeling somehow unrewarded. But the other parties were fun.

Everyone was asking me when Frank would be

home, and I would reply that that was a very good question. When he had left, he had expected to be gone only the improbably short time of one week. But his nice secretary at Bristol's, who kept me posted on the latest rumours, said that people kept thinking of extra things for him to do and extra places for him to go to, and phoning or cabling these bright ideas to him, so that his arrival-home date had gradually skidded from one day to the next. At this, I asked the nice secretary to promulgate it as widely as possible that if Frank's arrival date skidded one inch farther, I would need either to commit *hara-kiri* or move away, because he had faithfully promised the committee of the Hucklebury Revel (an annual event on the last Saturday in June, which, from its title, smacked of some of the more decadent days of ancient Rome) that he would be back home in time for him and me to judge the Kiddies' Fancy Dress Contest and give out the prizes. And that even though it had been made clear that the only reason we were invited was that in a community where everybody knew everyone else, we didn't know one child from the next, if Frank let us down, I wouldn't care to face the Committee, let alone the kiddies' mums. Being fed to the lions in the arena would be nothing compared to that!

The result of this impassioned plea to the tender hearts at Bristol's was that they immediately delayed Frank's return until the very day of the Revel.

When I awoke that morning, the sun was

shining (Mrs Smith had said that it always shone on Revel day), distant music was playing, brisk hammering was rat-a-tatting in the road below, fastening bunting to one of the floats for the parade, *and* our phone was ringing. I dashed to answer it like a mad thing, and it was, it truly was Frank, from London Airport. He sounded wonderful. A shade too calm to please me, but wonderful. I asked him when he'd be home, and he told me, and I immediately forgot what he had said, I was in such a tiz, and had to ask him again. He said two and a half hours. Whee! I asked him if he remembered that he was judging at the Revel this afternoon, and he said of course he did, he wouldn't miss it for worlds. When he had rung off, I just stood there and let the sun stream down.

That was at eight-thirty. At eleven sharp, the familiar big glossy black Company Humber with the fancy driver slid in at our gates, and there indeed was Frank. He looked browner and wearier than usual, and I think he had grown an inch or two, but otherwise he looked exactly the same. I asked him if he would have breakfast, or lunch, or even supper if he wanted to call it that, but he said he had already had several breakfasts, and what he really wanted was an hour or two's sleep. So that's what he had, with the whole village working itself up into Revel-itis outside.

At two-thirty precisely, there we both were, dressed in our best summer clothes, standing at our front gates to watch the parade go by. All the other villagers were at their gates too. Mr

Collingswood, the village constable, was looking very important and impressive, standing at the cross-roads with his white armband to stop any foreigners' cars which might inconveniently wish to pass through the village. From the distance, drawing closer, came the thump of military music, and, glory be, around the corner past the church came the carnival procession, led by the band of the 1st Hucklebury Boys' Brigade tootling and drumming away, a truly splendid sight. All the dogs in the village went wild and barked their heads off, and we villagers all cheered and stamped and threw our hats in the air. Behind the band came the decorated floats overflowing with children in fancy dress. You wouldn't believe there could be so many children in one small village. And their costumes, mostly home-made, were so good that Frank and I looked at each other in dismay, wondering how we could ever choose the best. The parade marched on, made a loop around the roundabout in front of the school at the next corner, then back it came, past our house, past the church and the post office again, then on to the recreation field, where the judging was to take place, with all of us following along, as the parents followed the children who were following the Pied Piper.

In our unenviable role of judging the best costumes out of so many good ones, we were greatly helped both by expert guidance from the committee, and also by there being so many prizes that no child went home empty-handed. There were eight different classes, divided according to age, starting with the under-fives, and for each class there were three prizes: first, five bob; second, three bob; and third, two shillings, with a sixpenny consolation for every child who had not won anything else.

Then there was the Punch and Judy Show, followed by free teas in the tent for all children of school age *resident in Hucklebury*, and a packed tea *outside the tent* (the italics are theirs) for children over twelve. Then we had tea with the committee. This was followed by the Children's Sports (on top of all that tea!), including, for various ages, the Potato Race, the Egg and Spoon, the Sack Race, and the Obstacle Race. Then came the Tug-o'-War (entry fee four shillings per team), the Handicap Race, and what was called the Slow Bicycle Race. I never discovered what that last one meant, because around then we both began to crumple and sloped off home, thus missing also the Revel Dance in the Miners' Institute (music by the Hucklebury Revellers).

When I had kicked my shoes off and Frank had brought us a nice cold dry Martini, the best I'd had since he went away, I got around to asking him about his trip. I asked him whether, in all his travels, he had experienced anything like the Hucklebury Revel. He said most emphatically that he had not.

Country Seat

Do work at my Country Seat ? No, thank you.
When I find a Country Seat, I sit in it.

G. K. Chesterton

For four days of the first week in July, Frank was in Paris.

The day he got back, a curious thing happened. The story of George and Skippy and the car key must have circulated around the Works (through Frank or George, certainly not from me). Because when a big shot in a California aircraft firm turned up in England and was invited down to Bristol's, and when, to everyone's horror, it turned out that he intended, as a matter of course, to bring his wife along, in the ensuing flap as to what to do with a female feminine dame in an all-male establishment, some bright soul, remembering that Frank had a genuine American wife who wasn't positively allergic to other American wives, visited Frank's office the very second he stepped into it from Paris, and after a certain amount of foot shuffling, came right out and asked him if he could persuade me to meet the wife off the London train tomorrow and take her anywhere, just anywhere, away from Bristol's. They would give us a Company car and driver for the day, and for lunch we were urged to go to the best restaurant we could find and go right down the right-hand side of the menu, choosing the most expensive items. I think if I'd worked it right they would have thrown in a few shares of Company stock as make-weight, they were that desperate.

But actually I didn't need any persuading. It sounded fun. The only reservation I had, which I offered on a platter for these men to consider, was whether two wives, possibly of different age groups, whose only common ground was that they were both born within the confines of the United States and were both women, would necessarily spark off that instantaneous *rapport* that the men expected of us, especially if one of us hailed from California and the other from Boston, and one of us was under the delusion that she was going to be spending the day with her husband. But the men didn't seem to think it mattered. I gathered that they were not planning to fritter the day away worrying about us.

They did however carry their gratitude to the point of providing *two* limousines and two drivers. The first car scooped up Frank and me at home and took us in to the station; I guess to make sure we got there. The second car drew alongside it in the station yard, and kept its engine running. The minute the unsuspecting couple emerged, Frank nipped out of the first car, introduced himself, steered Mrs V.I.P. smartly by the elbow into the car with me, introduced us, and left us with the classic conversation-stopper: " You two ladies speak the same language." Then the two men jumped into the other car and drove rapidly off, leaving the wife, the driver, and me holed up together for a long long day.

To start the ball rolling, I suggested a brief whirl around a few of Bristol's beauty spots. If these bowled her over, she concealed it well. I then asked her tentatively if she would like to go shopping. She said (and they were about the first words she had spoken, principally because in my nervousness I had been having a talking jag and hadn't let up for an instant), she cleared her throat and said that her husband always said that you could buy anything in the world on Wilshire Boulevard, and that they didn't plan to do any shopping in England. I then asked her if she liked museums. She said not particularly, and looking down at her pretty little feet, beautifully shod (from Wilshire Boulevard no doubt), I could well see that they wouldn't last out a museum very well. My next gambit was to ask if she was gardening-minded. She said she had a lovely garden in California, but that the gardens she had seen over here didn't seem to grow the same things. I agreed that there were very few palm trees hereabouts. This was good for a token smile between us through a wall of ice.

I still wasn't very worried because every American who had visited us so far had been a pushover for Bath, with all those Georgian buildings and all those antique shops, so I asked the driver to head in that direction. The only point I had overlooked was that a Californian isn't so much an American as a Californian, and the usual rules seldom apply. After my guest had politely stifled yawns right through the Pump Room and the Octagon Room, I could see that it was a dead loss, and that Beau Nash, Ralph Allen and the Wood family just needn't have bothered as far as she was concerned.

So after lunch (where we had no difficulty spending enough money to please the men) I cornered the driver and hissed to him that Bath was a washout, and could we please go to Berkeley Castle? He snapped a look at his wrist-watch and said he had been told to get us back to our house to meet the men by five p.m. sharp, but if we moved right along we could have half an hour at the castle. I said that would do fine.

To my intense relief the castle was quite a success. When we entered the great medieval banqueting hall, with the long table made out of a whole oak, and the minstrel gallery and all, my friend's face lit up and she said, " Now this is the sort of place I like. Some of our friends in California have a living-room just like this." And before you could say "Pacific Palisades", we were splitting our sides laughing, and I could hear the wall of ice cracking as it fell down.

It was quite a merry trip home. We and the driver got matey, and he told us one of his experiences driving people around. He was in the Bristol station yard in his best uniform and the car all shiny, waiting for the London train to pull in, when a pretty girl drove up alongside him, also waiting for someone, and they got to talking. She said she was meeting a friend of her husband's, whom she had never seen, and she didn't know how in the world she would recognise him. So our driver told her that he was doing a similar thing, meeting three men from London whom he didn't know, but that a sixth sense guided one on such occasions. At that moment, three men emerged from the station, and, without a word being spoken, the driver opened the door and the men climbed in. As he drove off, he smiled at the girl and she gave him the thumbs-up. When they were out of the traffic in open country, the driver caught the middle man's eye in the rear-view mirror and, without turning around, said, " Is this your first trip to Bristol's, sir? " " To where? " one of the end men asked, and added, " Good God, man. Aren't you taking us to the prison? " The driver stopped the car and looked back, and it was now perfectly clear that the middle man was handcuffed to the two other men. With a very red face the driver turned the

car and drove back to the station, where a black
Maria was by then waiting, and so were three
important-looking men. As they effected the
transfer, the pretty girl, who was still waiting
there, leaned out of her window and said, " What
about the sixth sense today? "

In spite of all the hilarity, we arrived home
sharp on five, just as the men drove in from the
other direction, and they were pleased with us,
which is always gratifying. Since then, this wife
and I have run across each other from time to
time in various parts of the world, and we have
become great friends, perhaps cemented by that
first funny encounter we had.

But I learned something from this small inci-
dent. Whenever after that the Company asked
me to convoy a woman guest for the day, and they
did so now and then, I always said yes when I
could, but with one simple stipulation, that I
could take along another, British, Company wife.
I am sure this was more pleasant for the guest, and
it was broadening for the rest of us. For instance,
there was the Hawaiian wife who kicked off her
shoes and did a sample hula dance for us.

Friday the thirteenth turned out to be a lucky
day for us. That was the day an assortment of
Hembroughs arrived to move the stone archway
to the end of the yew alley. We have a photograph that we treasure of three of them pretending
to hold up the arch like caryatids, after they got
it into the new position. They were with us a
couple of weeks, and at the end of it we all shook

hands just as enthusiastically as we had at the beginning.

On the Sunday, a nice sunny day, Frank had a revolutionary idea. He said why not get out some deck-chairs and just *sit* in the garden. We tried it and I was crazy about it. I said I wished we had thought of it earlier, say eight or nine months ago. Frank said that if we had, we wouldn't have much of a garden to sit in. Then he arose absent-mindedly and started to weed the lawn.

I had to admit that the weeds did look decidedly big as seen from a deck-chair, and I thought apathetically of bestirring myself to help him in his repetitive task. But I quickly stifled this impulse and determined I would *not* feel guilty about relaxing here thinking beautiful thoughts, the most beautiful of which was that most of the garden effects I was now admiring came not from repetitive, but what Frank called non-recurring, jobs. (Though, with Frank around, non-recurring jobs seemed to recur a bit too often for my taste.) Proving, if it proved anything, that given a bit of encouragement and a dollop of manure, Nature was inclined to be man's ally rather than his enemy.

Take that little alpine garden masking the giant beech stumps. Last time I had consciously looked at it, and not then with admiration, had been the day the mountain-climbing cow had mooed at me from its peak. Now, all by itself seemingly, it was a miniature upland meadow, carpeted in many colours. The big crescent bed, which we had so recently described as a semicircle of stakes stuck in the ground with labels flying, was all of a sudden a tight pattern of foliage and blossom, a real shrubbery. The hundred scrawny baby yew trees, which we had bunched miserably together and heeled in, during the December snows, and chased across a field in the January gales, had already thickened into a low hedge and were shooting up as fast as any schoolboy. The big rose garden, which Frank had divided with grass paths forming a cross, and which, in a rare moment of discouragement, he had once called a bed of weeds interspersed with occasional roses and grass, was now a glowing kaleidoscope of flowers.

It was all very pretty. But I lay back in my deck-chair, with the seat of Frank's trousers weaving in and out of my line of vision as he, viciously for one so gentle, stabbed dandelions and daisies with his sword-stick. And I wondered how in the world, since neither of us had ever been particularly hipped on gardening, we had got ourselves into such a situation. The most unwelcome feature of it, I mused, was how our London friends, whenever we showed our faces up there, exclaimed about how healthy we both looked, when I, for one, felt like a frail shadow of my robust city self.

It was true that any time I wanted to fill the house with flowers all I had to do was to take a long hike around the garden with basket and scissors, not much more of a hike than from the London mews cottage to the little florist around the corner, but probably quite a bit more expensive when you added it all up: the cost of the house, and of the builders to make it liveable, and the rates, and Mr Chilprufe's wages, and the capital outlay for plants, and whatever Frank's and my entire leisure time was worth; say five pounds per blossom? What of the vegetables that Mr Chilprufe was suddenly so keen to grow for us? What price would they come to: ten shillings per potato? Who was taming what? I asked myself. Were we taming the house, or was it taming us? The answer seemed as clear as it was disconcerting.

But I was no longer thinking beautiful thoughts, so I got up and helped Frank with the weeding, right through to supper time. The minute we had washed up, I fell into an easy chair and was asleep. When I woke up, Frank was laughing at me and saying it was bedtime. I told him dopily that I didn't think it could be healthy, exposing myself to all that fresh air. It was enough to make anyone feel morbid.

Also in July, I heard from the publisher. In the letter of mine that he was answering, I had apologised for not replying sooner, saying I was up to my ears in strawberries. In this letter he said, with admirable single-mindedness, that the strawberries might provide good material for my next book. This caught me at a particularly fraught time, and as I handed the letter to Frank, across the table at breakfast, I commented merely, " *What* next book? "

I wrote back that the simple country life didn't allow for such pleasures as book-writing, and I added, in further explanation, that we were preparing to evacuate the house for a week, so that a fumigation company could saturate it with cyanide, to eradicate death-watch beetle. To this the publisher replied serenely that the cyanide story sounded like a good episode for a book.

This summed it up. Because although the actual fumigation was still a fortnight off, the aura of cyanide seemed already to pervade all our activities. I told Frank I knew just how they must have felt at Westminster Abbey when they had to fumigate. There were so many tentacles to the problem that it was more like getting involved with an octopus than with a family of attractive little sturdy chocolate-brown, peace-loving, sun-worshipping beetles with cabriole legs.

The first casualty attributable to the fumigation was the state of the back wing of our house, which, until that was completed, had to stand empty, unpainted, unpapered and incredibly dirty.

Now there were the stone-masons. They were such treasures that one felt they would remain cheerful and competent to the very last moment, even if Noah's flood were closing over their handsome heads. But the fact remained that, barring miracles, they were not going to be able to finish their job by Saturday week, and were going to have to tote all that heavy gear away for fumigation week, and hump it all back in again in August.

There was also the small matter of suing the surveyor. This was now capably under way in the hands of our solicitor, who assured us that we need not start worrying yet, as the preliminaries might drag on for months before anything positive began to happen. Nevertheless on nights when I was over-tired I was apt to have this lurid dream in which for some unaccountable reason I was the only witness for the prosecution, and everything was going wrong, as in a Robert Benchley court scene.

But more palpable than any of this was the every-day burden of ruthlessly tearing apart what we had so recently and so tenderly assembled. We were all so zealous that in no time every room began to look like a disaster area. The garage was already so full of edibles and sleepables that there was no room for the car.

But let's not dwell on it. Let's turn to the nice part: Frank and Mrs Smith. Frank not only arranged to take the last three days off work, to pry up floor-boards and help with the heaviest lifting, he also fixed it that he and I would spend the week in our favourite Bath hotel, the Francis, and make a little outing of it. As for Mrs Smith, she almost convinced me that she regarded the drudgery of taking down curtains, rolling up rugs, and heaving heavy boxes around as fun. She also said she would really *like* to take part of her holiday the week we were away.

Quite aside from the fumigation, that Sunday turned out to be rather a full day by our usual standards: at noon, to a drinks party in the village; at one, to a luncheon party at another house in the village; at three, back to the house to hand over to the fumigation men; after that, to Bath, to check in at the Francis and put our

feet up briefly; and at six, back towards Hucklebury to a cocktail party in the next village.

So we got up early, put on dirty jeans, and after
breakfast and washing up, we moved the big
mattress and all the bedding from our bed, and
all the rest of the food, out into the garage. Then
for a bath, putting on good clothes, sitting on
suitcases, and off for the carefree social whirl that
our village abounded in.

When we returned at three, the fumigation men
had arrived and were pitching a tent on the lawn.
It looked rather festive, like a summer fête. The
minute we unlocked the door, some of the team
started carefully offloading the big sealed canisters
of hydrocyanic crystals and distributing them
among our rooms, the number of canisters to a
room varying with the size of a room. They told
us that after we left they would tip the crystals
onto newspapers and leave them to release their
gas gradually over several days. Another couple
of men were going around sealing our nice newly
painted windows and all the fire-places with
quantities of paper and Sellotape.

We could see that they were fidgeting to get us
out of the way, but I kept cooking up quite
superfluous last-minute jobs that I felt had to be
done. The last of these was when I exclaimed
loudly to Frank and the head exterminator that I
had forgotten to pack away the silver. The man
said patiently that it wasn't really necessary for
madam to do that. I said, " But what if some
tramp should get into the house? " The man
replied equably, " Well, that would be the end of

him, wouldn't it? " After this forcible point, Frank was able to lead me away quite quietly. So we never got to see the big red danger sign slapped onto our gates or the gate-sealing ceremony, but various villagers told us afterwards that it was pretty impressive and caused quite a stir, a sight to be pointed out to visitors, along with the church and the Miners' Institute.

We enjoyed ourselves so much in Bath that I really dismissed the house from my mind most of the time. When I did think of it, it was sort of preserved in aspic as it had looked in its prime. On Friday, when the head fumigator phoned us at the hotel to say that we could come home two days early, I was surprised by the lack of enthusiasm I felt at this prospect, but we pressed on and reached there about four. The head man greeted us, right on his toes and full of vim, and showed us around with such a proud proprietary air that I felt it was now his house, not ours, which was O.K. with me. When Frank asked him about the result of the fumigation, the chap let his fervour wane a bit. He made us feel that this was rather a disappointment. Now with Nelson's ship, he said, that was really gratifying, they had swept up jam-jars full of beetles in the cleaning up period. In our house he doubted whether they had scored more than a few hundred. I felt that we had somehow let him down, and told him so. " Not a bit of it," he assured me heartily, " it has been a very interesting operation." In thanking the team for their vigils, I asked whether they would now get a few days off to recuperate. But they said with obvious relish, no, they were going straight on to another job: a mill that had moths in the looms.

It was after they left that shock began to set in. The house was such an unholy mess. It was like seeing again, after long absence, a once robust and healthy friend who has had a long illness. And in spite of the tangible stamp of approval of the County Medical Officer, right there in our hands, that it was safe for us to return, and the wide-open windows blowing in God's clean fresh air, there was this sickly sweet smell of cyanide catching the throat and permeating everything. Could it be, I asked Frank, that the Medical Officer was merely keen to stamp and sign the paper so that he could get away for the week-end? Frank replied, with small comfort, that if so, he was probably well away by now, and that he, Frank didn't suppose that they had left us with a fatal dosage. The men seemed lively enough, he said; they were fairly bounding around. I said gloomily that perhaps that was a symptom.

After we had unrolled the bedroom carpet and hoisted the mattress and bedding back upstairs, and made up the bed with clean sheets, which I said firmly was all I was going to do tonight, Frank, to cheer us up, got out the makings of a martini from the garage, and we drank it, without ice (the men had told us to throw away the ice-cubes when we left and freeze new ones when we returned). We drank it sitting forlornly on a bench in the garden in the gathering dusk. Then I ferreted around the garage for some tins I could open for supper. As a gesture towards the civilised life, Frank chose a bottle of white wine from his bin in the hall cupboard. But it was a dreadful disappointment. It tasted strongly of cyanide, and we emptied our glasses down the sink. Frank said bleakly that it was obvious the system had slipped up here; in spite of their saying it was safe to leave bottled wines indoors, he would probably have to end up by tipping all the bottles down the sink. The thought of doing anything so strenuous tonight wore me out and I asked if he couldn't leave it until tomorrow. Then we went to bed. Even the toothpaste tasted of cyanide.

By the next day everything was better. Mrs Smith unexpectedly appeared (I had thought she was still away on holiday), and with her came Mrs Smart. They were in rip-roaring form and told us to leave it all to them, and they did a super job, putting everything back and polishing each room until it shone. They said they were going to start on the back wing next week. And it was a good thing Frank hadn't thrown the rest of that bottle of white wine down the sink, or any of the other bottles in his bin, as he had meant to do last night. Because it turned out that it was only our taste-buds that had been full of cyanide; the wine we had drunk and the food we had eaten were perfectly all right. I know because I tried a smidgen of wine right after breakfast, and it tasted fine.

China to Peru

Let observation with extensive view
Survey mankind, from China to Peru.

Dr Samuel Johnson

Frank was planning to fly to South America the second week in August. I put it that way because he *was* to have flown to India briefly the previous week, a few days after we returned from Bath. He had a great rush getting his cholera shots and having his white dinner jacket cleaned (he was travelling rough!) and at the last minute the trip was killed dead, which was fine with me.

This time the great idea was for quite a little gang of the *élite* to take the new Britannia (or it

would take them if you prefer) and tool around
the Americas in it, and there was some ugly talk
about their returning via Singapore and Australia
if the mood struck them. They must be (I quote)
back in Bristol before the end of August to attend
the agents' conference. This was billed to continue
for a week, bringing us to the Farnborough Air
Show, also lasting a week. For the following week,
apparently nobody could think of anything special
to do, except maybe rest up for the third week
in September, when an important international
air conference was to take place in Edinburgh.

Here is where I step into the picture because, to
my astonishment, all those quaint little wife-tours
of mine suddenly bore fruit, and the Company
actually *invited* me to accompany Frank to
Edinburgh, not only all expenses paid for a week
in a four-star hotel, but they were also driving
Frank and me up there in a Company limousine,
with a driver who happened to be an old friend of
mine from previous expeditions. I asked Frank
with narrowed eyes what the catch was, and he
opined that I was supposed to give the glad eye
to the wives of any American or other foreign
blokes who turned up in Edinburgh and steer
them daintily away from under the men's feet.
I asked Frank what language I was supposed to
decoy the foreign wives away *in*, reminding him
what my French was like, and he replied gallantly
(at least I hope it was gallantly) that my French
would enliven any gathering.

By now the itinerary for the South American
tour was taking shape. It included such places

as Mexico (Frank was calling it Mehico already), Habana (Havana to stay-at-homes like me), Jamaica, Bogota, Caracas, Panama, and of course (quote) B.A. (unquote) and Rio, not necessarily in that order. The trick was that they were supposed to arrive as fresh as daisies at each new port of call, to prove to the natives how restful it was to fly by Britannia. The tour started: Bristol to Madrid, to Lisbon, to Madrid (I forget why), to the Azores, and points west.

Another Company wife and I went to see them off, which was not a terribly good idea from the viewpoint of a wife's peace of mind, because we weren't allowed aboard and the male members of the seeing-off party were; and they brought to us, as we stood with clean waving handkerchiefs at the ready, the gladsome tidings that the plane was awash with a galaxy of gorgeous Cuban air-hostesses, as a goodwill gesture. Goodwill to and from whom? We wanted to know instantly, but all we got was a great big horse-laugh from the men, who added, superfluously as far as I was concerned, that these girls had been chosen because they were the best in Cuba. " Best at what? " was our reaction. I told the other wife that I wasn't going to start worrying about it because in my view the problems attendant on a full-scale romp in an aeroplane would prove unsurmountable, however willing both parties. But she replied gloomily that it was a mistake to underestimate one's husband's capabilities in a challenging situation, and that anyway the trouble with planes was that they landed too often.

Then the plane took off and we waved until it was out of sight.

When I got home I felt unaccountably restless and couldn't settle to any form of activity. I tried going to bed early, but that didn't work either, so I read late, and woke up late, and felt dopy. That day I didn't have any trouble keeping busy, especially with the whole Smith *ménage* in full spate in the back wing. In fact I worked so hard that I had trouble not to fall asleep over supper. I must have been in bed by nine and asleep five seconds later.

It was two a.m. when the phone rang. As I struggled awake to answer it, I was full of anxieties, but it was all right. Boy, was it all right, it was ruddy wonderful. It was Frank, speaking from Bristol! He sounded remarkably bright and cheerful, and very casual. He said something had gone wrong with the plane's radio in Madrid, and they had decided to fly home to have it repaired properly before the long South Atlantic crossing. He wanted to know if he could bring a fellow-traveller back to the house for the night. " Male or female? " I wasn't too sleepy to ask. Frank said it was a man of course. I told him I would be happy to arrange it. They turned up so quickly that they helped make up a bed and get out drinks and food, and the occasion had all the makings of a good party until we all started yawning cavernously, and hit the hay.

Frank had been fairly rushed on his first departure, with packing and all that, but this time he had until evening to kill, and he used a bit of it on a sort of C.O.'s inspection of the garden, telling me what jobs I could be getting on with in his absence. I was still so effervescent at having him back so unexpectedly that I humoured him in treating me as the under gardener and didn't even consider any back-chat. And even after he had gone again (I didn't see him off this time; I told him I wouldn't make a habit of it if he was going to keep popping back), and I had gone upstairs to put old jeans on, it still seemed to me to be a sort of Sacred Trust to hurry right out into the garden, mustard keen, and do exactly the jobs that my Loved One had laid down. This exalted mood unfortunately didn't last very long, what with the sun getting ready to set and all those midges, especially as from where I was squatting in Frank's yew alley, the height and profuseness and infinite variety of the weeds were inescapable. There were even some full-grown lupins in the grass.

At that moment there was a whish of sound in the sky above, more a whisper than a noise, and over the house, quite low in the sunset, the Britannia, with Frank aboard, flew past. It flew right down the path of Frank's yew alley, its shadow skimming me as I stood up and waved and waved until it was just a speck in the distance. I couldn't see whether it was quite gone yet because of my foolish tears.

By this time you probably won't fall in a faint if I tell you that Frank didn't get back to Bristol on the date planned. For one thing the Britannia, in its busy busy life as the toast of the Latin-

American countries, was three days late in returning. My spies at Bristol's had kept me fully informed about this, and a kind friend had actually stopped by to pick me up for the landing ceremony. This was quite an excitement, and I wouldn't have missed it for anything, and I got a pot of geraniums out of it that had decorated the plane's lounge. The only drawback was that Frank wasn't aboard. No one had thought to mention this in the numerous cables that had been floating around between the plane and the Company. Those aboard knew about it, of course. I mean they hadn't just mislaid him while crossing the Atlantic without any one noticing, or anything like that. They all assured me that he was alive and well, was doing an extra job that had been thought up for him, and would fly home by commercial plane, nobody seemed to know, or care particularly, when. Somewhere along their route they had ditched the bevy of beautiful Cuban hostesses, and I sought assurance that Frank wasn't shacked up with one or more of them on some lovely tropical island. But all I could get out of his colleagues was that if he had this in mind, he hadn't mentioned it.

So I went home again, with my new hat on but minus one husband. The next thing that happened was a perfectly splendid cable from Frank, from Rio, saying:

' LUFTHANSA PLANE DELAYED STOP TRANS-
FERRING SAS ARRIVE LONDON AIRPORT 1035
SUNDAY VIA FRANKFURT '

As this was the first I had heard of any plan involving Lufthansa, it added to my frothy feeling that life was indeed a spicy affair: today, Rio; tomorrow, Frankfurt; next day, maybe Hucklebury!

Thus it was that on the first Sunday in September, sharp on one o'clock, a Company car delivered Frank to me all in one piece. What with his sleeping it off, and unpacking from Rio, and repacking for the Farnborough Air Show tomorrow, I didn't really get his undivided attention until drinks time, when he emerged and asked me if I'd like a martini. With that important point settled, I enquired about his trip. He immediately embarked on a long story concerning a Brazilian nightingale (bird not opera singer)—a sort of myna bird, that a man, another passenger, had in a cage all the way from Rio via Frankfurt to London; how this chap had rented a hotel room in Frankfurt for the brief stop-over time, especially for the bird, so it could fly from the window into the park and back again for exercise; how in Rio, where the man bought it, it had quickly picked up all the new songs in the carnival procession and could sing them back to him; and how this man had a flat overlooking Regent's Park where the bird could disport itself when it felt like it.

Fascinating though it was, I eventually wrenched Frank loose from his bird and asked him, among other things, whether in the course of this trip he had become expert in dancing the tango with a rose between his teeth, and he said no, that Latin America didn't seem to be doing the tango much this season; that it was all the samba, the rumba, the mamba and the cha-cha-cha. He then described a few of the night-spots which their hosts had rustled up for them, and for a brief moment we both did silent reverence to the glories of high life in the tropics and sub-tropics. Then Frank visibly pulled himself together and, with somewhat belated but no less welcome chivalry, added that he was really a very home-loving type, that all this gadding about could be a bit of a bind, and that he was never so happy as when he was leading a quiet life here with me. " It is sweet of you to say so, darling," I replied, " and most reassuring. It leaves only one tiny obstacle to our complete happiness together: I don't think that *I* am the home-loving type."

Unfortunately he didn't seem the slightest bit worried.

Here's to Orgies

Home is heaven and orgies are vile,
But you need an orgy, once in a while.

Ogden Nash

During Farnborough week, Frank passed briefly
through our house several times, usually on his
way somewhere else.   He was due home from
Farnborough " latish on Saturday ", whatever that
meant.   Latish on the Friday he phoned me from
the show, not to tell me that his return was to
be delayed, which I fully expected, but to say that
he had just run across our dear Canadian air
marshal, and had asked him down to stay with

us, Thursday until Saturday. I said, "Wonderful, darling, but isn't Saturday the day we leave for Edinburgh?" Frank said that's right; that the air marshal would be leaving for Edinburgh in another car about an hour before we left. He started to ring off, and then added, as an after-thought, that he had been told to tell me that I would need two ball gowns at Edinburgh and as many cocktail dresses as I could muster. Then he did ring off. He said someone was waiting for him.

That week in Edinburgh was all it was cracked up to be. There was a reception by the Lord Provost in the Council Chambers; a Tattoo with pipe and military bands and sword-dancing on the esplanade of the Castle; a dinner-dance at the George Hotel, at which Bristol's were hosts; and a ball at Hopetoun House, seat of the Marquis of Linlithgow, with the Latin-American band of Edmundo McRos (as we always called him thereafter) and a comely display of Scottish dances. That wasn't the end of it, by any means. During the day, the object of our all being there was the series of highly technical conferences by and for the men. And at nights, in between the big events, smaller events sprang up, so numerous that one host had to wedge his champagne party in at midnight, which by then seemed quite a normal thing to do.

A thing I wasn't quite prepared for was how Scottish the Scots can sound on their own terrain. I had promised myself that while I was on my publisher's doorstep, I would phone to thank him for his nice publishing. I got around to this, egged on by Frank, right after lunch on the Monday. A wee Scots lassie answered the phone, and when I asked for the publisher, she said, " Ach, he's awa'." When I asked how long he would be awa', she replied that he was only awa' to his dinnerrr. So he phoned us back, and Frank snatched half an hour from his meetings to go with me to call in at their beautiful Georgian offices, where plenty of *real* writers, from Sir Walter Scott to Sir Compton Mackenzie, had been before me, and all in all it was one of the delights of the trip.

There weren't all that many American and other foreign wives present at Edinburgh, and what Continentals there were spoke a lot purer English than I did, so my French fortunately remained untested. What *was* present was a tiny little moo-eyed South American millionaire, whom Frank had run across in his travels under the spell of what local customs I dread to think. He and I had barely met when he started cosily nibbling my hand and tentatively pinching me (*not* on the hand). Then he would scamper his fingers up my arm to the shoulder, tweak my ear, and blow at me as if I were a horse.

I had had little training for this sort of thing, and the language-problem again loomed large, the only Spanish phrase I knew being ' *si, si* ', which was the last thing I wanted in this crisis. I looked big-eyed at Frank for guidance, hoping he might any minute offer our guest a choice of weapons in support of my virtue. Not a bit of it.

To the millionaire, a potential customer of Bristol's, Frank's attitude was a wholesome, tolerant approval of his peccadilloes, as we call them in Spain. He sat there smiling and nodding encouragement to us both, in a manner later described by an onlooker as, " Go ahead, have another nibble. Help yourself to a pinch and a tweak. Be my guest."

As the ball wore on, the millionaire, who by now was carrying a massive load of champagne for one so small, took to following Frank and me around the floor as we danced, keeping in step with our sedate progress. Suddenly he snatched me from Frank's arms (at which Frank instantly retired from the field), drew me to him, and, embarking on some intricate Latin steps performed on a dime, he first flung me away and then yanked me toward him until, my eyeballs rolling in their sockets, I thudded against his chest with a loud smack. Then he bent me backwards over one arm, waiting for me to snap.

By now the other dancers had relinquished the floor to us, and our particular friends, or as such I had hitherto regarded them, were, along with Frank, wiping their eyes with merriment. Having more room to play with, Valentino branched out and began running in circles around me, snapping his fingers and flapping his coat, as if he were a matador and I the bull. As a finale, he twirled me around several times, and while the world was reeling, he grabbed my arm and spun me off. I skidded, caught him in the instep with my high heel, tripped him up, and he went down as flat as a dead mackerel. He made one supreme effort to rise, thought better of it, and lay there on the floor, with a beatific smile on his face, humming a little tune along with the band, while keeping time with one upturned pointed shoe. After a bit, two extra-large South Americans, apparently his henchmen, came and shovelled him up and carried him off in a business-like way—just part of the day's work. And that was the end of my Valentino. I never saw him again.

When we arrived home from Edinburgh, I immediately foresaw that I might require a brief period of adjustment to tide me over from the world of free champagne and caviare to the workaday world of crops and manure. Not so Frank. The minute we had stepped out of the car, bidding the driver a grateful farewell, Frank changed hats and became that lovable rustic character, the rural squire. This wasn't an act on his part, he *was* it. He took pleasure in the vegetables that had been going to seed in his long absence from the scene: the lettuces, beans, corn, squash and broccoli; he reported these to me as being in not bad shape, and asked me what I'd like him to pick for supper. He also reported that the grapes in the vinehouse were rapidly ripening, and he brought us in some big luscious bunches of both black and white to try. They were simply delicious. He said he thought we might try selling a few to the Hole in the Wall. He took some over to the Smiths, to congratulate them on their super job of painting and papering the back

wing. At the same time he asked them if next
week-end they could help us pick and store apples,
of which there were large quantities on the trees,
and with their usual good humour they agreed.
But Frank said that first we must ask the County
Agricultural Adviser to come over to tell us what
varieties we had, and what their keeping qualities
were. He went straight off and phoned the
adviser, who agreed to come next Thursday
evening, so that Frank could be there too.

Among the letters awaiting our return was one
from our solicitor, concerning our law suit with the
surveyor, which had seemed to reach a stalemate,
the surveyor refusing to budge. To help things
along, I had phoned our solicitor just before we
left for Edinburgh, to say that, following a
suggestion of his, I had gone right through the
house, front and back, to compare it with the
survey, and had noted down any errors in the
document, whether major or minor, but all costing
us money. The solicitor was now saying that he
had reported this to the other side; that they had
appointed an independent surveyor to call at the
house for an inspection; that I should go over-
board giving this independent chap all possible
assistance; that as soon as possible after he left,
I should make a detailed written note of everything
that happened, including what I had shown him,
what questions he had asked, and what replies
I had given; that such a written note would be
admissible as evidence in the witness box (back to
my dream again!) and that he, our solicitor, now
had great hopes that our case would never come

to Court. (So did I!) Frank phoned the solicitor straightaway, and between them they set the date for the inspection for Thursday morning, the same day as for the County Adviser. So I really felt I was right back in the saddle of a bucking bronco called Hucklebury House.

As for the back wing, Frank said he was toying with the idea of not letting off that wing to tenants, as we had sort of planned, but instead getting in a full-time experienced gardener and his wife to live in the back and grow straw-berries commercially for us, starting with our own half-acre, and if that paid off at the end of a year or so, to plough up the two-acre field. He said that meantime we might buy some geese to keep down the grass in the old tennis court. and perhaps a dog to protect the geese from foxes. It all seemed absolutely crazy to me but, won by his warming enthusiasm, I patted him and told him he was marvellously adaptable. " Yes," he said thoughtfully, still absorbed in these plans, " in a way it's a pity that I have to go to Israel next Sunday." I told him that this was what was known as breaking it gently. I told him I would have to put butter on his paws to keep him at home more.

That night I had another dream. It was about the herb garden, one of Frank's paper projects, which he had been running over with me that evening. It was to be at the left of the yew alley. In the arid space where the rosemary and sage and chives and marjoram and so on, given us mostly by helpful friends, then sprawled, Frank

223

visualised it, some day, as a formal herb garden, cut into segments by twill-patterned brick walks, like the ones at Hatfield House, converging on a Regency well-head (still to be found), to cover the well I found last winter.

In my dream, the herb garden was finished. And what a garden it was! It was set in our surroundings all right, with our walnut tree on the left, and the big apple tree over to the right, and the high stone wall and the Hembroughs' archway behind. But everything was much more glossy and tidy than in real life. The brick paths were laid in a wonderfully intricate way, with fragrant well-trimmed box hedges running beside them, all centering on a beautiful well-head smothered in climbing roses. There was something vague about Royalty coming to see it, and that seemed easy and desirable too.

In the morning when I woke up, it was still so real that I half expected it to be out there, transformed overnight by some pantomime fairy queen. It wasn't. I took a peek and all I found was Mr Chilprufe regarding the couch-grass disconsolately.

After breakfast I told Mrs Smith about my dream. She took it calmly, as she took everything. " They do say in the West Country," she said, " that if you dream something on Friday night and tell somebody about it on Saturday morning, it is sure to come true." " Heaven forbid! " I exclaimed, fully aware by now of the hard work involved in making that kind of dream come true.

Happy Ending?

Life's a pudding full of plums, . . .
Life's a pleasant institution,
Let us take it as it comes !

W. S. Gilbert, *The Gondoliers*

Autumn had come around again. We had been
in the house just over a year. The newspapers
were saying again that it was the coldest this and
that since 1947, but in our part of the world
Hucklebury House was as warm as toast. The
apples were stored and labelled. We were picking
and eating the last of the grapes, and tidying up
the garden for the long winter ahead. Frank,

who had just returned from Stockholm, soon after his Israel trip, was talking of buying a hundred baby Christmas trees to grow commercially in the bit of field that Mr Chilprufe had just finished clearing for us. The back wing of the house still stood empty; we had written to all the nearby farm-schools offering our proposition, but nobody had leapt to it, and we were reverting to the old idea of having a tenant. This week we had sent particulars to the main house-agents, and had already had several nibbles, nothing final. As to our law suit, the surveyor had at last succumbed to our solicitor's patience and skill, had agreed to settle out of court, and was now dickering in fairly large terms through our solicitor over the exact amount of damage we had suffered. Our three or four builders' bills were coming in one by one, and each time we winced where it hurt. Altogether they totalled a good deal more than we had paid for the house. And the County's housing cheque, which we had, at last, received (and which, according to those expensive leaflets, had been supposed to cover half our conversion costs to a maximum of four hundred pounds), amounted to the munificent sum of twenty pounds, returnable to the County if we sold the house within ten years.

On one of these autumn mornings, Frank phoned from the office with an astounding proposition. He talked in such a low voice that I had to ask him to speak up. He asked me how I would feel about moving away from Bristol. I told him the idea made me wild with excitement. I said it was just like old times. At first I didn't even think to ask where we might be going, and when I did, Frank dropped his voice again, and I could just hear him say that we had better not talk about that on the telephone; that he could tell me that it was a Continental capital that we had visited but never lived in (which covered practically *all* the Continental capitals); and that he thought we would like that part of it. As to the job, he wasn't so sure. He would try to find out more. He said he had to go now; he was due in a meeting three minutes ago. He said we'd discuss it tonight. And he was gone.

I walked blindly out to the garden, sat on a bench and lit a cigarette. I found to my chagrin that I was trembling. It was absurd. Here I was, a reasonably well-integrated civilian wife, with the only possible husband, an almost equally enviable house, and enough friends nearby to keep anyone happy. What possible excuse was there for me to go all to pieces like a travel-mad adolescent at the mere mention of the word " Move! "

All day long I was caught in a web of dreams— selling the house, packing, finding a place to live in the new city, wherever it was. The day flew. Evening came, and Frank arrived home. He was in fine spirits and went straight off to mix us a drink.

I raised my glass and said questioningly, " To the new job? "

" Oh, that," he said. " I thought it over and decided we'd be better off here."

I was flummoxed. " What do you mean, better off here? " I asked, trying not to sound like a

227

fishwife.

He said, " Oh, you know. It would mean uprooting us entirely. And the job. At first it looked very grand, with plenty of perks, and it paid better than this one. But when I examined it more closely, it didn't seem like a full-time job at all. Not half as interesting as my present job. And I don't suppose either of us really wants to leave this house, just as we've got it looking so nice."

I sat and stared at him with my mouth open and realised with mounting dismay that he was getting attached to this house. It was no longer a simple asset, like stocks and shares, to be sold lightly and unemotionally. If I didn't watch out, it was going to be one of the family. We weren't playing for fun any more. We were playing for keeps. If I wasn't extremely careful I might find myself spending the rest of my life in this delightful photogenic friendly village bounded by open fields.

I came to because Frank had broken off in the middle of a sentence, something about his future plans for the house. " Is there something wrong? " he asked solicitously. I told him not to give it a second thought, I was just a little disappointed that we weren't moving, but I'd get over it. " Why? " he asked me. Wasn't I happy here? I told him I was happy as all get out, but that I didn't want to spend the rest of my life here. Frank said there wasn't any question of that, that he knew of. I told him I found the house fairly demanding, with him away so much and all.

He said he knew we'd had a tough year here, but that he hoped things would be easier now, and that the house would prove to be just a nice background for normal living. I laughed ruefully and said I didn't think this house had the least intention of being a ' background ' to anything. I said it had been foreground stuff for a century and a half, and that it wasn't likely to surrender the upper hand at this late date.

Neither of us said anything for a bit. He put out his hand and I took it. He asked me if I'd like to go on a trip to America next time he went. I said I'd love it. He said there was something he hadn't meant to mention yet because nothing was settled, but that there was already some talk about a conference at Monte Carlo next spring or summer, and of their cutting me in on it, the same as at Edinburgh. He asked me if I'd like that, and I said I would, I would. Then he said it was still fairly light in the garden and he'd like to go out and do a little work there, if supper would wait. I said it would, and that I'd join him.

It was beautiful out in the garden. The air was crisp and hazy and there was a whiff of bonfires. The house looked touchingly lovely. Deceptively fragile and ethereal. A swag of late blush-pink crinkly climbing roses brushed the sun-warmed grey stone wall of the front façade, and swung lightly in the evening breeze. Looking the other way, the eye still caught the massed brilliance of the herbaceous borders that we had worked so hard over. This was the house, this the garden, that had looked so old and frail and tired and docile and asking for protection when we took it over, and that had proved to be so solidly set and thick-walled and stubborn once we began to try any changes: the house that I came to the West Country on my little high heels and with my citified ways to tame to my mould, and that ended so easily by taming me.